100 Ideas for Secondary Teachers:

Literacy Across the Curriculum

Graham Tyrer

BLOOMSBURY
LONDON · OXFORD · NEW YORK · NEW DELHI · SYDNEY

Bloomsbury Education
An imprint of Bloomsbury Publishing Plc

50 Bedford Square	1385 Broadway
London	New York
WC1B 3DP	NY 10018
UK	USA

www.bloomsbury.com

BLOOMSBURY and the Diana logo are trademarks of
Bloomsbury Publishing Plc

First published in Great Britain 2018

Copyright © Graham Tyrer, 2018

Graham Tyrer has asserted his right under the Copyright, Designs and
Patents Act, 1988, to be identified as Author of this work.

All rights reserved. No part of this publication may be reproduced or
transmitted in any form or by any means, electronic or mechanical,
including photocopying, recording, or any information storage or
retrieval system, without prior permission in writing from the publishers.

No responsibility for loss caused to any individual or organisation acting
on or refraining from action as a result of the material in this publication
can be accepted by Bloomsbury or the author.

A catalogue record for this book is available from the British Library.

ISBN
PB: 9781472950239
ePub: 9781472950246
ePDF: 9781472950222

2 4 6 8 10 9 7 5 3 1

Typeset by Newgen KnowledgeWorks Pvt. Ltd., Chennai, India

Printed and bound in UK by CPI Group (UK) Ltd., Croydon CR0 4YY

This book is produced using paper that is made from wood grown in
managed, sustainable forests. It is natural, renewable and recyclable. The
logging and manufacturing processes conform to the environmental
regulations of the country of origin.

To find out more about our authors and books visit
www.bloomsbury.com. Here you will find extracts, author
interviews, details of forthcoming events and the option to
sign up for our newsletters.

*For my Mum and Dad who helped me love language.
For my daughter: may your love of words never end.*

Contents

Introduction	ix
How to use this book	x

Part 1: Assemblies and tutor time — 1
1. Beginning sentences in tutor time — 2
2. Tutor room library — 3
3. Tutor group newsletter — 4
4. Emotional literacy wordbank — 5
5. Literacy roll call — 6
6. Forum theatre — 7
7. Story assemblies — 8
8. A play for assembly — 9
9. Language skills assembly: punctuation and conjunctions — 10
10. Language skills assembly: paragraphs — 12
11. Language skills assembly: Standard English — 14
12. Language skills assembly: reading examination questions — 15
13. Language skills assembly: writing examination answers — 16

Part 2: Literacy in the community — 17
14. Website promoting language skills — 18
15. Parents' evening literacy advisers — 19
16. Class pairing — 20
17. Year 6 literacy display — 21
18. Pride piece — 22
19. Literacy in the neighbourhood — 24
20. Governors' learning walk — 25
21. University links — 26

Part 3: Literacy in the library, corridors, social spaces and staffroom — 29
22. Staff literacy noticeboard — 30
23. Break time support club — 31

24 A visiting author	32
25 Speakers' corner	34
26 Word trails	35

Part 4: Supporting disadvantaged students, those with SEND and the more able **37**

27 Helping parents in the community	38
28 Supporting reluctant writers	39
29 Withdrawal session for disadvantaged students	40
30 Find – Infer – Name – Deduce (FIND)	42
31 The full stop in five minutes	43
32 The full stop in ten minutes	44
33 The full stop in over ten minutes	45
34 Writing about subject knowledge	46
35 Writing about understanding	47
36 Punctuation challenge	48
37 Experimenting with prepositions	49

Part 5: Developing student leaders **51**

38 The emotional literacy leader	52
39 The greeter	53
40 The chair leader	54
41 The learning to learn leader	56
42 The literacy coordinator	58

Part 6: Training staff and promoting literacy in staff meetings **59**

43 Literacy is a shared responsibility	60
44 Team approach to spelling	61
45 Student literacy presentations	62
46 A homework plan is a literacy plan	63
47 Research extracts	64
48 Planning grid	66

Part 7: Lessons – all subject areas **69**

49 2–3–4	70
50 Description warm-up	71
51 Three tokens	72
52 Listening with the whole self	73
53 Mnemonics	74
54 Cloze activity for keywords	75
55 Look, say, cover, write, check, use	76

56	The inventor of words	78
57	Word continuum	79
58	Modelling the online thesaurus	80
59	Build a thought	81
60	Beginning, middle and end	82
61	Joining two sentences	83
62	Linking ideas, encouraging precision	84
63	One word leads to another	85
64	The order of things	86
65	Self-assessment quadrant	87
66	Word limits	88
67	The 'the' challenge	90
68	T cards	91
69	C scripts – try before you buy	92
70	C scripts – writing	93
71	The power of alliteration	94
72	The power of simile	95
73	The power of metaphor	96
74	The rule of three	98
75	Punctuation for all	99
76	Subject – Time – Event – Place – Suspense (STEPS)	100
77	Dance or mime the facts	101
78	Hotseating	102
79	Analyse the diagram	103
80	*Dragons' Den*	104
81	Plenary page	105
82	Ambassador oracy	106
83	Preparing for a learning walk – literacy	107

Part 8: Lessons – maths 109
84	The Frayer grid	110
85	Comparison in mathematics	111
86	Mathematics reading	112
87	Mathematics vocabulary grid	113

Part 9: Lessons – science and technology 115
88	'Thinking words' in science	116
89	Invent an element	117
90	Writing for clarity in science	118
91	Sounding formal in science	119
92	T cards for exam preparation	120
93	Build the content	122

Part 10: Lessons – art, drama, music and PE   **123**
94 The punctuation party   124
95 Vocabulary in art   125
96 Punctuation in music   126
97 'Thinking language' in PE   127

Part 11: Lessons – PSHE and history   **129**
98 Persuasion in PSHE   130
99 Conjunctions in history   131
100 Questions in PSHE   132

Introduction

This is a practical handbook for both secondary teachers and leaders of cross-curricular literacy. Literacy is a shared responsibility, so the ideas I suggest are suitable for all subject teachers, pastoral teachers, form tutors, school leaders, heads of department, librarians, governors and leaders of cross-curricular literacy.

I offer advice for building literacy into the everyday life of your school. The ideas are designed to promote competence and confidence. I want to support you in your daily teaching and help you make cross-curricular literacy an everyday reality. You can adopt or adapt the ideas to suit yourself.

I also want to support you in your busy life. You may only have time for a glance or a skim through this book, but in these ideas I want to give you enough to prompt a thought, to start a conversation or to connect to something you've seen in the classroom today. The book is a companion to your thinking. I hope it will challenge and reassure you.

I want to encourage you to build on what you do every day rather than make wholesale changes. For example, building literacy into assessment, offering written challenges as part of homework, improving behaviour by developing the language of leadership, giving students access to classroom libraries, and using parents, other students and the governing body as real audiences for students' writing and reading. Above all, I want to help you make literacy manageable.

Dip into this book whenever you need help, when you're planning a lesson, a display, a scheme of work, a training session, a team meeting or a parents' event. Use it every day or just use it some days. Use it when you need it for inspiration, suggestions or evaluation.

Literacy is for life. I hope these ideas will help your literacy teaching every day, everywhere.

How to use this book

This book includes quick, easy and practical ideas for you to dip in and out of, to support you in teaching literacy across the secondary curriculum.

Each idea includes:

- A catchy title, easy to refer to and share with your colleagues.
- An interesting quote linked to the idea.
- A summary of the idea in bold, making it easy to flick through the book and identify an idea you want to use at a glance.
- A step-by-step guide to implementing an idea.

Each idea also includes one or more of the following:

Teaching tip
Practical tips and advice for how and how not to run the activity or put the idea into practice.

Taking it further
Ideas and advice for how to extend the idea or develop it further.

Bonus idea ★
There are 18 bonus ideas in this book that are extra exciting, extra original and extra interesting.

Online resources also accompany this book. When online resources are referenced in the book, follow the link, www.bloomsbury.com/100-secondary-LATC, to find extra resources.

Share how you use these ideas and find out what other teachers have done using **#100ideas**.

Assemblies and tutor time

Part 1

IDEA 1

Beginning sentences in tutor time

'This is perfect for a form tutor wanting to help students to build their confidence in written tasks and to notice how they begin sentences.'

In examinations, it can help to get to the keywords of the answer close to the start of the sentence. Completing this simple activity in tutor time will help your students practise beginning their sentences in this way.

This is a pastoral activity that focuses on a real audience. Here, the audience is the writer. Give each student in your tutor group a blank piece of paper and ask them to write a letter to themselves. Explain that they will open it in a week's time.

To help students write their letter:

- Have them describe four places in the school. It might be three classrooms and the break area.
- Next have them write about four times of day. For example: tutor time, first lesson, break time, a lesson they usually find difficult, on the bus home.
- Teach them that it is important to have the reader imagine *something happening* or *something sensed* as early as you can in the sentence.

An example would be:

There is a reading book in my bag. I have my pens with me because I got organised before I left home. My friends are kind to me and ask me how I am. I do the same for them. Then the bell goes. I feel nervous but I stay strong and tell myself I'll try hard; that's all anyone can ask.

Teaching tip

Turn these pieces of writing into real letters. Seal them in envelopes and return them to students to open a week later. On the envelope, write, 'Only to be opened on [date a week from today]'.

Taking it further

The following week, have students write a similar letter to a partner. Begin by having partners talk about what they would like to happen in a week's time. It gives a pastoral opportunity for students to discuss short-term goals. It also helps to remind students that effort can be as important as achievement.

IDEA 2

Tutor room library

'This is for any form tutor who wants to promote the pleasure of reading.'

Reading is an essential skill in every subject in the secondary curriculum and as a form tutor, it is important to raise the profile of frequent and regular reading among your students.

Set up a part of your classroom as a lending library. It works even if it's just one shelf or book box. Ask the school library to supply you with a range of fiction and non-fiction every six months.

Make good use of the library throughout the school year by:

- Setting aside 15 minutes each week for private reading. Students can bring in their own books or choose from the tutor library.
- Modelling your own private reading. Many students find it encouraging to see adults reading and hearing adults talk about how they choose books, what to do when they get stuck and how to stay focused. Bring a book in of your own and read this while the students read theirs. Don't worry about requiring quiet for you to do this.
- Discussing with students how to make a book selection by 'warming a book up' through reading the blurb and the first few pages and by looking for recommendations from book lists or book reviews.

Taking it further

Have a part of your tutor wall devoted to book responses. These can be in Tweet format, email layout or letter form. They are better written to the tutor group.

IDEA 3

Tutor group newsletter

'Even if you publish a newsletter just once a term, you're helping develop a literacy habit.'

A tutor group newsletter reinforces the importance of writing for an audience. Some students find this helpful when subject teachers reinforce the importance of drafting and being accurate.

Suggest to your tutor group that they publish a tutor group newsletter. Start by inviting students to publish one per year. They may well do two or three. The newsletter should only be one page of A4. The aim is to keep the writing succinct. The skills required in their school writing will draw on this: writing accurately, with economy and relevance.

To publish a more regular newsletter:

- Ask students what roles they'd like to take: news writers, sports reporters, theatre correspondents, art reviewers, letters page, fiction section, feature writers. This can be useful as an ongoing Social, Moral, Spiritual and Cultural (SMSC) project throughout the term.
- You should be the editor-in-chief. You have the final decision over what's attempted, planned and written. There is obvious British Values learning here: how democracy works and how the impact of students' writing needs to be considered before publication.
- It's always helpful to let other relevant staff know what you're doing; heads of year, for example, may want to link what you're doing with their planning for the pastoral programme.

> **Teaching tip**
>
> You might publish the newsletter on the year group intranet. Getting constructive feedback or even dialogue with the reader helps some students want to improve their style and accuracy.

IDEA 4

Emotional literacy wordbank

'If you're a form tutor you can help students grow an emotional literacy wordbank.'

You can help students become curious about the differences between emotion words. This will help their literacy and also help them to think about healthy emotional responses to events.

- Have students keep an 'emotion list' in their planners.
- You could add to it occasionally by using an online thesaurus. You might model for them how to use the thesaurus, having the class suggest some emotion words and discussing the alternatives.
- Use the list of emotion words in the online resources. Turn them into cards. Have students see if they can group them, turn them into hierarchies, opposites, pairs or a spectrum. Words will change position or relationship to each other depending on context. Students typically say something like, 'Well, it depends what's happening'. This is a positive thing; what we want to encourage is a nuanced approach to context.
- Have students put the words into three boxes: 'I know what this means', 'I don't know what this means', 'I'm not sure'. Then, students say why they made their choices. There will be agreement and disagreement; sometimes you'll just want to put students right when their guesses are obviously incorrect.
- Ask students to try out the words, test them in three-minute role plays and challenge each other to try them in everyday life. This is what we want to supportively develop: the structured growth of vocabulary.

Teaching tip

The three-minute role plays might be about encouraging supportive behaviours, students helping each other cope with difficult homework, what to do if they get 'stuck' or helping a new student who seems lost at break.

Taking it further

You might use the words to develop imaginative writing for a tutor language wall. This could include haikus, extracts from scripts, short stories or 'how to help one another' ideas.

IDEA 5

Literacy roll call

'This is a very quick activity to build subject vocabulary. Try using it to make a literacy event out of taking your lesson register.'

Many students enjoy 'bringing to life' the technical terms lists they often see displayed in their classrooms or in their books. It helps make the keywords more memorable and encourages students to use them in their own writing.

When you're taking the register, ask students to reply using a subject vocabulary word instead of the word 'present'. To do this:

- Ask the students to research a name or process that begins with the first letter of their first name or the name they reply to in the class register.
- This can also be a grammatical term, a type of verb, a place name, a technological material or a modern foreign language phrase.
- When a student's name is called, they reply with the technical term. Of course, if the school policy is that only particular phrases must be used in reply during register taking, you drop a separate literacy roll call into the lesson at some point. The benefit here is that you're drawing attention to language when students least expect it. Some teachers find this an even more effective way of doing it.
- A display can be made of these technical words celebrating the work that went into the activity. Having played the game, the display now has a different resonance.

Taking it further

Instead of researching a technical term, have students think of the name of someone who achieved something noteworthy with the same initials as their own. There's an element of curiosity here, as students will want to know more about someone who may be relatively unknown.

Bonus idea ★

Students find the most obscure element, process, grammar term, foreign language term, scientific process, musician, artistic skill or whatever relates to a subject they know well. They then invent one, making sure it sounds convincing. During vocabulary register, you invite students to give fact or fiction and have the class challenge any they doubt.

IDEA 6

Forum theatre

'This helps students' literacy by getting them to see what differences changes would make and experimenting with a range of vocabulary and grammar.'

To improve your tutor group's spoken language, try engaging them in this activity. It will help them work out what to say in difficult situations before they arise and it will also enable them to see the effects of certain words and phrases.

Think of some tense situations that might arise for students in your tutor group. For example, a student doesn't quite understand the homework or an explanation given by another student or the teacher. How does the student ask for help, particularly if they're feeling shy?

Have the class suggest a list of phrases that might help. These could be phrases the student says out loud or those they say in their head. They could be questions for the teacher to ask that don't make the student feel embarrassed but make them feel encouraged. You act as scribe, writing phrases on the board. Accept helpful phrases and open up discussion about which would be more useful.

Try improvising the scene with a volunteer using the phrases on the board to help. The class can suggest other phrases as the drama goes on.

Taking it further

Students could offer to take the place of you or your volunteer to take the scene further. By raising a hand, they can stop the improvisation. They then suggest a different phrase to help the scene. They take your place or that of your volunteer to develop it further.

IDEA 7

Story assemblies

'Story assemblies can be inspiring for students and provoke curiosity about literacy.'

Offering students a monthly fiction focus in tutor time will help them to be curious about fiction and regularly incorporating this into assemblies will encourage all students to invent, wonder and guess about fiction.

Engage your tutor group in an activity that focuses on story-writing and if possible, encourage all the tutor groups in a year group or all the classes in a subject year group to do the same. Keep the activity small. Make it doable in, say, fifteen minutes. Then, invite small groups of students to give five-minute presentations to their peers in assemblies.

Try having a sequence of, say, four fiction focus tutor groups. Have students respond to any of the following prompts:

- Opening lines: invent opening lines for books that haven't been written.
- Endings: write the last lines of stories no one has yet read.
- Titles: imagine titles for books that haven't been written.
- Front covers: design covers and write blurbs for books yet to be written, by authors no one has heard of, from publishers you invent.
- Cliffhangers: write three cliffhangers to end chapters in mystery, science fiction or crime stories no one has yet written.
- Missing word lines: challenge students to supply possible words in sentences from imaginary stories, poems or plays.
- Characters: think up characters that haven't found a story yet. Give them strange sounding names and impossible characteristics or commonplace names with unusual histories.

Teaching tip

You could also have students invent mysteries looking for a solution or think of myths that belong to imaginary civilizations and explain why rain falls, why the sun shines, why air is invisible, how thunder happens or what makes lightning.

Bonus idea ★

Book club: One of the keys to success is suggesting it lasts for, say, half a term and meets, say, three times. Help students to feel successful even if they only meet once.

Silent reading rooms: Some students enjoy knowing that on a certain day in the week, one tutor room will be open at lunchtime for silent reading.

IDEA 8

A play for assembly

'Help students' literacy by getting them to write a short play for an assembly presentation.'

Asking students to write a short play to act out to their peers in an assembly promotes writing for effect and provides an incentive for drafting and accuracy (especially if the script is to be given to others to read and if the script is to be published). Writing, performing and watching plays relating to the curriculum can also help lesson content become memorable.

When asking students to write a play for assembly, keep the rules simple. For example:

- The time limit is three minutes.
- There must be no more than three characters.
- Try writing the last line first.
- Try beginning with an argument.
- Try giving each character no more than five lines.
- Try strict turn-taking: first one character, then the second, then the third.

You could model this activity for the students. You provide the opening line, a contentious claim, perhaps, and ask students for the next line. You might ask all students to have a go at the next lines in their books, then pair students up to share them and develop the play further.

Teaching tip

Characters can be allegorical to help relate the play to curriculum content: past, present, future; quaver, crotchet, stave; infrared, ultraviolet, visible light. The play could be spoken mime: for example, the orbits of planets, a group photograph illustrating the most influential historical figures in a key event or a key transition in geographical time.

Taking it further

Publish the script online as part of the student writing library on the school's website (see Idea 14).

9

IDEA 9

Language skills assembly: punctuation and conjunctions

'Using assemblies as lessons can help you get consistent literacy messages across to the whole year group.'

Literacy assemblies help develop a shared understanding of key language skills used across the curriculum. They are also a practical way of putting into action a plan to teach all students the language techniques you have decided are important. Assemblies also offer an opportunity for non-specialist staff to be reminded what certain language terms mean and what their function might be.

Teaching tip

Use whatever texts inspire you. Communicating your enthusiasm helps teach language skills. Students often prefer to be given a genuine document that is in use for real purposes.

This literacy assembly focuses on punctuation and conjunctions. Start the assembly by showing students an image (available in the online resources) of the Cassini-Huygens mission, 93 million kilometres in space, taking a photograph of the moon Europa, where, it is suggested, the conditions for life may exist.

Instead of immediately explaining what the image is, try using a sequence of questions like:

- What does the image make you feel? Imagine? Think?
- What does the publisher want you to do?

Then reveal, with the enthusiasm you feel, where the image is from. Invite a science or technology teacher to share his or her enthusiasm. Then show the text relating to the image (see online resources). Give a little background. The text is from the NASA *Launch Services Manual*. It describes, from one engineer to another, how to construct part of a Saturn V launch vehicle. It tells someone how to build a component that will help the rocket gain escape velocity (5 miles per second from the surface of the earth).

Finally, reveal a close-up of the text. Showing a detailed accessible extract helps do the following things:

- Students will recognise the language features they've been studying since Year 4 (commas, semicolons, full stops) and see how they have been used here to help launch a spacecraft.
- Students will see the use of conjunctions and the fronted adverbial. They can get a reminder that these words and phrases have helped open up an idea, connect ideas and allow an engineer to assemble the spacecraft.

Invite the science or technology teacher(s) in the assembly to use the same sequence of image and text in their teaching. They have been given a resource that helps in at least two ways:

- It helps students get cross-curricular reinforcement of the school's teaching of these key language skills.
- It helps students see how there is a relevance to these skills both in different subject disciplines but also in a context that, in this case, takes humanity beyond our planet.

Taking it further

All colleagues thus have the opportunity to link this activity to their own teaching, for example, teaching skills for answering the GCSE science six-mark answer. When students can associate what they've been taught earlier in an assembly with what they learn in the lesson, many find it helps in building their recall and retention.

IDEA 10

Language skills assembly: paragraphs

'You might find there's relief from staff in the assembly. Almost all staff want there to be a clear definition of paragraphing. It gives everyone a shared teaching language.'

This activity introduces students to the STEPS acronym as a way of paragraphing (see Idea 76). It works in every subject, so it's a good technique to teach a whole year group in an assembly.

Teaching tip

You might want to play some music during the assembly, using a microphone for yourself and student volunteers. A little theatricality makes the content memorable. It also works to use staff as volunteers, which students enjoy watching.

Explain to students that you change paragraph when you change:

- **S**ubject
- **T**ime
- **E**vent
- **P**lace

or when you want **S**uspense.

Now show a text with the paragraphing removed. It helps if you choose a text from a website that students are likely to be unfamiliar with and that relates to something current. You could use, for example, an extract from this article about the Cassini-Huygens space mission: **https://saturn.jpl.nasa.gov/news/2939/cassini-begins-epic-final-year-at-saturn/**

Students work in pairs for two minutes on a task like:

- What kind of paragraphs will this text have? Line spaces or indents?
- Where is the most obvious place for a break?
- Is there a change of subject or place or action or time or suspense?
- What about after '...F-ring orbits' or after '...Pasadena, California' or after '...(2,400 kilometers) wide'?

All three of the suggested places in the last task example count as subject change and action changes. This is the point. There are many places where paragraphs might be included.

When you show the actual piece, the students will see there are not only paragraph breaks but also section breaks and bold subheadings, line breaks and caption inserts. Explain that the text has been shaped to have an improved effect.

> **Taking it further**
>
> Try having four teachers from four different subjects show an example of writing in their subjects. Concentrate on paragraphing and have each teacher say why the paragraph breaks came where they did. This might be because it helps order the content or help an examiner award marks more easily. It might be for both reasons.

IDEA 11

Language skills assembly: Standard English

'Assemblies are so good for getting consistent skills messages across to your students.'

Standard English will help students achieve success in examinations and formal situations. It helps to be clear about this and to remind students that Standard English is needed throughout their writing lives.

Teaching tip

Standard English is also known as Standard Written English (SWE) and is the form of English most widely accepted as being clear and proper. Remind students that Standard English is especially helpful when writing because it maintains a fairly uniform standard of communication. It needs to be understood by all speakers and users of English regardless of differences in dialect, pronunciation and usage.

Bonus idea ★

Challenge students to investigate the history of Standard English. A good place to start is *Mother Tongue: The English Language* by Bill Bryson (Penguin, 2001). You might also have students investigate and report back on other forms of English.

Role play a job interview for a teaching position in an assembly. Have a student play the interviewer. Just add some dialogue that very obviously isn't Standard English. For example:

'Good morning.'
'Good morning.'
'How are you?'
'I be very well.'
'Would you like to work here?'
'I wants that very muchly.'

Next have students talk in pairs about their reaction. Then use the projector to write the script of the next exchange. Have a student write up suggested lines from the assembly. Ask how the teacher might get a bit further in the interview if he/she wants to impress the headteacher. When the students have agreed suggestions for the next four lines, play them out. Ask how they might be further improved.

You may find that most students are keen to have the candidate use effective dialect without you prompting anything. If they suggest verb forms that lack agreement, offer an edit.

IDEA 12

Language skills assembly: reading examination questions

'This idea will help students grow in confidence when reading exam questions.'

In an assembly, we can help students see how reading skills can be transferred across subjects and how important these skills are in examinations. Show students how skilled readers get over their nerves. Offer them a structure when they see a tough question.

Offer students three questions from three different examinations – for example, mathematics, science and English. This process alone helps students see basic similarities in examination questions, including how we have to establish the number of marks available, how the questions are written in the same formal, Standard English voice and how they require efficient time management.

Ask teachers from the relevant subjects to read their subject question and think aloud as they do so. Students need to hear how you can overcome stress and how you read forwards and backwards. Too many students are under the impression that a good reader reads in an unbroken linear left-to-right flow.

Next, apply steps and ask questions based on the FIND technique (see Idea 30):

- **Find** the most important words in the question.
- What do you think the examiner wants you to show? (The '**Inference**' step.)
- Which words could not be found in any other subject? (The '**Name**' step.)
- Which subject skill will you need to use more than any other? (The '**Deduction**' step.)

Teaching tip

Remind students that practice is key, particularly frequent mindful practice.

Taking it further

Ask, 'Which words could be edited out of the question?' Spending a few minutes having students challenge each other's responses to this helps them understand the form of the question.

Ask, 'Which words help hold the question together?' This helps draw attention to the 'grammatical words'. Prepositions and conjunctions are often used in mathematics and science in subject-specific ways different to, say, English.

IDEA 13

Language skills assembly: writing examination answers

'A great assembly idea for a teacher wanting to get a consistent literacy message to a whole year group.'

Assemblies can be an efficient use of time to teach economy, efficiency and answering directly, which are essential to succeeding in written exams.

Begin the assembly with a warm-up activity. Ask students to list all the objects they can see from where they sit. They have 30 seconds. Their partner has a turn. They can use any of the same objects. Can they find more? Say they will score a point for everything they can find.

Discuss how much content can be described in such a short time. It's usually more than students think. Ask them to notice how economical their talk was; they probably didn't use many unnecessary words. Ask them to notice their tight focus on the question. Ask them to recall how they wanted to do better next time. All these skills can be transferred to exam writing.

Next, model an answer to a multiple-mark question in your subject. Show them key writing skills. As you write, speak aloud your self-editing. Ask students to notice the balance between grammatical words (prepositions, conjunctions, articles) and lexical words (content, subject-specific words).

Teaching tip

Ask students to notice the way you have started sentences. You may have used the keywords of the answer. You probably haven't used 'the' as a fronted adverbial.

Taking it further

Draw attention to the use of shorter sentences, the use of commas to separate ideas and secure marks. You might show how the semicolon can be used to list points, especially when the question asks for a number of reasons, causes or features.

Part 2

Literacy in the community

IDEA 14

Website promoting language skills

'Your school website can help prioritise literacy in the minds of students and families.'

Try having a tab on your school website that clicks to examples of students' writing. It can be an effective means of publishing students' work and motivating them in their writing.

Teaching tip

Have students make suggestions for the future of the site. How could it provoke curiosity for learning? You might be able to hyperlink to the fiction tabs of other schools, including your partner primaries. You can also build a sense of community writing by inviting your staff to contribute short pieces of fiction.

Arrange with whoever manages the school website to include a tab in the site's navigation dedicated to students' writing. Upload work edited and written by your class, year group or tutor group. Edit, of course, and check what they've written is appropriate before posting it, but what better way to emphasise the need for accuracy? It makes marking purposeful, and students see the point of the writing tasks you set and are more willing to write correctly and effectively.

This written work could include stories, non-fiction (speculation about the future, poems, limericks, jokes, opinions about the past, celebration of diversity, games, reviews, letters) or writing for real audiences (parents, other students in the year group or class, governors). Have audiences guess whether they were the intended audience. These texts could also be used for study in future lessons.

Have students regularly review the contents of the site, being constructively critical about its layout, design and content. This makes a useful citizenship activity. Make them aware of the legal requirements for a site. Make them aware of the safeguarding policies keeping them secure.

IDEA 15

Parents' evening literacy advisers

'It's important to let parents know that there's help available for language learning.'

Try asking teaching assistants to have a 'literacy station' at your next parents' evening. They can be supported by students who share best reads and tips for spelling or getting punctuation right.

Asking teaching assistants and students to run a 'literacy station' at parents' evening will:

- Signal to parents that there's help available for language learning.
- Help parents support learning at home.
- Suggest just how much the school values curiosity about books and writing.

With guidance from the teaching assistants, 'student advisers' or 'literacy leaders' can give students and parents their experience about:

- how they learn spellings
- how they check their work for accuracy
- books they've read that they can recommend.

Often students attending parents' evening will be pleased to get reading suggestions from their peers, as much as from adults.

You could also invite parents to share their best reads. Have a book wall, staffed by the librarian and his/her helpers. As they wait for their appointments, ask parents what they would recommend to others, what helps them in their work and whether they've got any great lines or characters that stay in their memories. By the end of the evening, you might have enough parent and student book recommendations to post onto the school website as a record of the evening and as a resource for others.

> **Bonus idea** ★
>
> Why not invite your local bookshops to bid for a space? This needs considering with the governors but it helps independent bookshops survive; they might offer discounts and they would definitely spread the message about reading. Make sure you give parents notice if you decide to do this. You could also ask your local library to make an appearance and publicise what they have to offer.

IDEA 16

Class pairing

'Even if students exchange writing or reading once during the year, it gives them an opportunity to write for a reader or to learn about language from a different perspective.'

If you know a colleague in a different school, try linking two of your classes as real audiences. Students don't have to exchange names or other identity information. They can share views, perceptions, opinions, ideas and stories.

Once a year, pair two classes in different schools and ask all students in both classes to produce a piece of written work that will be exchanged with students in the other class. Try saying to your class, 'We're going to have someone your age in a different school read your writing. They might even write back to us. Think about how to be clear in your writing. When you check it through, read it as if you were the recipient.'

Students could write for the paired class:

- explanations of science processes
- opinion pieces on historical events
- poems, stories, non-fiction analysis
- points of view pieces about current affairs.

The students in the paired class each receive a piece of student work to read. They can then write back to share their own views and opinions.

Note: As with any links with audiences outside school, there's a due diligence and safeguarding role to be undertaken by responsible adults. It's worth discussing the requirements with your designated safeguarding lead. The gains are worth this necessary work.

Teaching tip

Students might also exchange learning materials, PowerPoint slides, weblinks, reading lists, revision techniques, acronyms and ways of organising time.

Taking it further

You could hold a Skype call between the paired classes, projecting it onto the screen so that it looks like the paired class is next door. Planned well, students can give short presentations that they've written about key events in their school, achievements they want to share and points of view.

IDEA 17

Year 6 literacy display

'Displaying some Year 6 literacy work when students come for their transition visits can encourage a sense of belonging and pride in their writing.'

It helps transition if Year 6 students see their work on display in local secondary schools. It doesn't have to be the school they're going to. Many students feel their writing is important if it's displayed in other schools.

Invite your Year 6 teachers to have their students write 50-word pieces of fiction, short poems or extracts of science writing and send them to you. Share this work so that upcoming Year 6s see it as soon as they come into the school. Have display boards at the main entry points with A1-sized writing done by one of your partner primaries for maximum impact. Single sentence montage displays help get as many students' work represented as partners wish.

Invite your art department to work with these pieces and later in the year present the artwork during a visit to the school. Invite students who know they are coming to your school to read these and some other pride pieces (see Idea 18) during transition weeks. If possible, get photographs of the display taken and sent to the partner primary.

Note: As with all liaison and display work, encourage best practice safeguarding. Let your designated safeguarding officer know what you're doing. Ask for advice on how this encourages a safeguarding culture.

Taking it further

Put some of this work up in the staffroom or circulate it on the intranet. It helps colleagues to know what kind of work is being done in primary schools. It develops relationships with partner primaries if colleagues know there's a regular sharing of what's being done.

IDEA 18

Pride piece

'This activity helps Year 7 students feel valued. And you have a great means of tracking literacy progress.'

Many students have information that transfers with them when they move from primary school to secondary school. Often, however, this information is only stored centrally. Try getting an example of each student's work from Year 6 in the front of their Year 7 exercise books on the first day of term.

Having a piece of the student's writing in the inside front cover of their subject exercise books can be a significant help as they transition between Key Stage 2 and Key Stage 3. Make arrangements so that when the students open their exercise books in September, they see a piece of work from Year 6 (or even Year 5) stuck in the cover. Here's how:

- Start the process around March. It takes a few months to organise but it's completely worth it.
- Ask the Year 6 teachers to spend the period March through to June choosing or even producing a piece of writing that both they and the student are proud of.
- It can be about anything and can be fiction, non-fiction, poem, prose or drama. It's better if there is some element of it that shows off punctuation variety, paragraphing, and spelling, but pride is the most important feature. If the writing had an effect on a reader or the writer or if it's somehow memorable, then it's very valuable for this activity.
- In July, you collect the pieces from the primary school.
- Then have the office copy these onto sticky labels and have them put in the inside covers of as many subject exercise books as you can.

Teaching tip

Teachers can use these written pieces to monitor progression of a child and a group and can refer to them in their verbal and written marking of the book, praising the progress made and challenging students to improve still further. Literacy leaders can make scanned copies for a progression log compared with work done later in Year 7.

- Teachers can see what the child is capable of so they can support, challenge and plan for progression. Often the piece makes more sense than a grade, score or sub-level.
- Tutors can use the piece as a conversation starter. Students feel their work from last year is valuable. They can talk about what they achieved in terms of the spelling, punctuation and grammar.

Taking it further

Consider transferring praise pieces from Key Stage 3 to Key Stage 4. Many students find it helps to start Key Stage 4 with new teachers by having this literacy link.

IDEA 19

Literacy in the neighbourhood

'Writing for a local employer can provide an incentive to check work for accuracy. It also helps build a positive perception of the world of work.'

Make contact with a local employer and ask them if they'll read some work done by your students. As well as supporting literacy, this can be a way to build positive relationships between the school and local businesses.

Ask the local employer if they'll tell your students what writing, reading and oracy skills they use and value in their employees. It can be a surprise for students to hear how, for example, someone they think they know well needs the same skills taught in school. Have students devise a questionnaire to use with, say, three employers they know to find out more about literacy skills needed in the world of work.

Next, invite students to write on such themes as:

- what I think the future of work will be
- my dream job
- why work is important to me and my family
- the business I want to own, one day
- the differences between work and school.

Then send these written pieces to the employers and ask them to feed back. The feedback might be verbal, communicated back via the teacher or written.

Note: As with all links to the community, seek advice from your school's designated safeguarding officer. Your school will have helpful policy guidance on how such links can contribute to the safeguarding culture.

Teaching tip

Invite careers, information advice and guidance colleagues to discuss with students the literacy needed in employment and in job applications.

Bonus idea ★

Ask students to design a guide to behaving appropriately with local neighbourhood employers. What should neighbours expect from students at the school? What are safe practices for students to and from school? Students might revise a guide to looking after their friends when they're out of the school environment, on the bus or cycling and making sure they get to school safely.

IDEA 20

Governors' learning walk

'Governors want to play a role in shaping the strategy of the school.'

Have governors come with you on learning walks a couple of times year so they can see the literacy project in action.

Invite governors to join you on a learning walk, making sure you keep the learning walk focused on a specific group of students, for example, disadvantaged, more able or Year 7 – whatever happens to be the priority focus of the literacy policy. Between you, the governors and the headteacher, you will gain a sense of what works and you'll work out together what to improve. Enlisting governors will make it much more likely that you'll have a chance to put your ideas into effect.

Try:

- Letting the governors see the challenges and successes.
- Encouraging them to conduct structured interviews with students.
- Suggesting to them straightforward questions that can provide information to help you and the students, such as:
  - 'What books are you reading?'
  - 'Do you enjoy reading?'
  - 'What writing do you enjoy?'
  - 'What writing do you find difficult?'
  - 'What has the school done that you've found helpful in your reading and writing?'
  - 'What do you think we could do even better?'

After the visit, have the governors prepare a presentation to the governing body. Planning this with them builds the relationship. It keeps the school consistent in its approach. It helps the governors draw on evidence rather than anecdote.

Teaching tip

It's good practice to discuss with the headteacher any work you do with members of the governing body; governors will want to talk with the chair of governors before beginning a learning walk. It's also worth discussing this with your designated safeguarding officer. Governors will want to make sure they are helping the school's safeguarding culture.

IDEA 21

University links

'This kind of link helps your students' aspirations when they get a positive view of higher education.'

Try linking with a university or college education department as a real audience. Trainee teachers will often have the time and incentive to read and give feedback on your students' written work.

Teaching tip

As with any links with audiences outside school, there's a due diligence and safeguarding role to be undertaken by responsible adults. It's worth discussing the requirements with your designated safeguarding lead.

Students' accuracy is likely to improve when they know someone is going to read their work. It helps students see that marking and assessment are essential parts of project and ideas development in settings other than schools. Invite a university education department to suggest trainee teachers to give responses to students' writing. Responses must be constructive.

Ask your audience to use phrases like these when they give feedback:

- 'This made me think of…'
- 'This made me curious about…'
- 'What if…'
- 'Imagine…'
- 'The three parts of this I liked the best were…'
- 'What you might consider next is…'

Some students might find it helpful to see the same response phrases used in school, such as 'even better if', 'what worked well', 'however'. It's supportive of the school's marking policy.

Have students review your school's marking policy. Give them 5 minutes at the start of the lesson or the start of a test. Have them say whether any sentences in the policy might be better expressed. You can't promise to make changes, but you can invite the author of the policy to visit the class and explain what they meant. It is frequent, low-cost activities like these that keep literacy on pupils' 'radar'. We need them to be thinking about literacy and the need for accuracy in everything they read and write.

Students might write about:

- incredible inventions
- imaginary countries/cities/towns
- predictions for the future
- solutions to historical mysteries
- myths from imaginary cultures
- alternatives to high energy consumption
- movie proposals (the trainee teacher responds as a producer)
- technology solutions (the trainee teacher responds as a potential investor).

In return, higher education students might offer reading lists of books that inspired or motivated them when they were at school.

> **Bonus idea** ★
>
> Invite a relevant university subject department to offer advice on revision, motivation and stories about how difficulties are overcome. Some universities are keen to get their own students to improve their writing skills by doing this. There's also a 'widening participation' expectation for most higher education institutions that supports this too.

Part 3

Literacy in the library, corridors, social spaces and staffroom

IDEA 22

Staff literacy noticeboard

'Displaying students' work reminds colleagues what these students can do. It may be surprising and prompt conversation across departments.'

Keep a literacy display in your staffroom or on your staff intranet. Focus it on the latest literacy skills you're teaching across the whole year group or school. Offer teaching tips, links to useful websites and examples of students' writing.

A literacy display in the staffroom is a way of keeping the value of literacy visible and 'doable', and it reminds teachers what their students are capable of across the curriculum. Most staff appreciate reminders that save them time. So, consider only having a maximum of three or four items on display. Consider changing them once a term.

Examples might include:

- The three key parts of the marking policy on a single side of A4.
- A list of best reads for disadvantaged students.
- Language learning strategies devised by students.
- Lists of books staff might enjoy, recommended by the librarian.
- A reminder of the most easily made spelling errors and their correct spelling.
- A photocopy of an exercise book before and after spelling work.
- A piece of extended writing by a student typical of a priority group in the school and representing expected progress given starting points.

Taking it further

Try offering extracts from a lesson plan showing how literacy has been built in. You could also display a scheme of work, a photograph of a classroom library, a list of literacy starters or websites for subject-specific style guides.

IDEA 23

Break time support club

'Getting older students to help run support clubs can help visiting students feel a little more confident.'

This idea involves hosting a break time drop-in support session for students. Some students like having something constructive to do at break and enjoy taking part in, attending or being guided to attend a skill session.

Over the course of a half term, host six support sessions run by a rota of staff or, ideally, staff and post-16 students. The sessions might focus on one core skill or on a range of skills found to be needed through work scrutiny.

Students attend through drop-in or through invite. If they are invited, it might be more effective to invite peers too to make it more social. You might want to introduce rewards for attending, such as a raffle ticket that gets put into an end-of-half-term draw.

Try adopting a time-efficient model like **imagine – imitate – invent**, in which students watch the teacher (or post-16 student) model a writing skill. This might be: how to begin sentences with words other than 'the'. Here's how it works:

- The teacher thinks out loud and the student **imagines** themselves doing something similar.
- Next, the student **imitates** what they've just seen. They might talk out their thinking to a partner or to the group on the whiteboard.
- Finally, the student **invents** a sentence independently and gets constructive feedback.

Teaching tip

The student might improve a sentence from their exercise book in a subject other than English. They then invite their subject teacher to make whatever comment, verbal or written, they want. It demonstrates a willingness to improve and commitment to the subject.

Taking it further

The student keeps track of the sessions they attend in their planner. They show these to their form tutor and parents or carers. The school communicates with home, rewarding the student for attending and for effort.

IDEA 24

A visiting author

'Getting a published author in to speak to your students can be life-changing for them. You don't have to look too far. You'll be surprised how many published writers you have amongst your staff or in your parent group.'

Invite a published author into your school to speak to a class or year group. The outcomes of the visit can be presented to all students in the library and publicised around the school.

Asking a published author to speak to your students can help encourage the pleasure of reading, develop knowledge about writing and the publication process, and enable students to see themselves as future published authors. Here are some ways you could ask the author to interact with your students:

- **Page 1 reads:** Students read the first page of each of the author's books. Students work on the first two sentences of the next page. They then compare this with what was actually written. Differences are celebrated.
- **Dramatic presentations:** For example, write short, one-page scripts bringing to life key moments in the author's work.
- **The author becomes her/his characters:** Ask the author to be a character from the book and hotseat with open and closed questions.
- **Top ten reads:** Ask the author for her/his reading history, fiction and non-fiction.

Invite colleagues in other departments to use the visit to help learning in their classes too. For example:

- **Textiles:** Students make designs for character costumes.
- **Design technology:** Students design inventions, objects and settings in the author's writing.

Teaching tip

Consider inviting non-fiction authors. Doing this helps students associate reading with a range of subject areas and not just English. Also consider inviting the authors of the local community websites. Interview them about information they publicise. What motivates the decisions about the history presented? What makes them select the local facilities illustrated? Interview them about their editorial choices, their web design and the language styles used.

- **Geography:** Students write about the settings of key events in the author's stories, their features, resources, benefits and protection needs.
- **History:** Students interview characters from the books as if they were primary sources to key events. They ask about reasons for decisions, influences on them and their relationship with other characters and social groups.
- **Mathematics:** Students compare the syllabic length of the words used in the writer's work with non-fiction to see if there are any differences and similarities that can be represented graphically.
- **Art:** Students design alternative covers for the writer's works.
- **Science:** Students investigate how the paper was made, where the ink comes from, how the ink stays on the page and why the book has its specific size and mass.

All these outcomes can be presented as part of a week-long display in the library and publicised around the school and on its website.

> **Bonus idea** ★
>
> Students write five-page novels, design the covers, write the blurb and publish them. Students hold launch events for their books in the library. Invite short talks from the authors. Interview the writers and publish them, according to their wishes, around the school and (in accordance with the school's safeguarding policy) on the school website.

IDEA 25

Speakers' corner

'These "pop-up" literacy events need careful planning but they help create a sense of "literacy everywhere".'

Writing for real audiences encourages students to pay attention to effects. It encourages curiosity, debate and discussion. Work with small groups of students to put on impromptu performances and readings around your school to support this.

Teaching tip

Suggest the presentation must have a strict word limit. If students are shown how to choose the most effective 100 words, they're learning the skills required in examinations to edit while they write. They'll see the teacher modelling how to balance grammatical with lexical or content words.

Ask students for suggestions for suitable sites in the school for impromptu performances. These can be lunch areas, tutor rooms, safe areas of corridors or entrance foyers. (Make sure you check them out. Everything we do must enhance the safeguarding culture of the school.) Performances can be unannounced. This adds a sense of drama, occasion and surprise – all positive features of language use.

Examples of subjects for the performances could include:

- points of view speeches about change in the world
- poetry readings
- descriptions of the future for technology
- paired role plays about keeping safe online
- interviews with students about their achievements
- advertisements for upcoming productions or events
- speed debates about current affairs issues
- performed questions to make people curious
- extracts from books that students find interesting
- radio plays involving characters from history, geographical experts or influential scientists
- sales pitches for time- or energy-saving technology
- invitations to students' art exhibitions and interviews with the student artists as if they're celebrities or prize winners.

Taking it further

Scripts used in the performance are posted to the website. A wider audience is reached. Students feel their work has more reach and that's another incentive for checking accuracy.

IDEA 26

Word trails

'This is a quick activity that gets students to focus on vocabulary. The key is little and often.'

Ask students to nominate an interesting or unusual word from a book they are reading. Put this on display in the library as a trail word for other readers to be on the lookout for in their reading.

Looking out for particular words promotes reading concentration, and paying regular attention to unusual or new words helps students remember them and develop an interest in vocabulary development. Exploring how a word may be used in different ways in different texts results in a richer, more layered understanding of language and recognising word family links supports spelling and the decoding of new vocabulary.

To support this, try building word trails to display in the library:

- Students nominate an interesting or unusual word from a book they are reading.
- This word is displayed as a trail word for other readers to look out for in their reading. Decide how long each word will be featured on the word trail, perhaps fortnightly or half termly.
- Students are rewarded using the school reward system if they find a trail word.
- The word finds are recorded by listing the title, author and page number of each book featuring a trail word.
- The words could become part of a curriculum challenge and subject teachers could incorporate them into lessons and/or reward students for using them accurately.

Taking it further

Display word finds as a trail through the library, linking together the locations of different books where the same word has been used, either as a physical display in the room or on a map-style handout. Invite library visitors to follow a word trail and report back what they find out about the word through doing so. Reward readers for completing a trail. Readers could also identify related words and build a word family tree through trail finds, which you can add to the display or reader map.

Part 4

Supporting disadvantaged students, those with SEND and the more able

IDEA 27

Helping parents in the community

'Many parents appreciate support as part of parents' evenings.'

Sometimes parents' evenings are focused on matters of routine. You might want to include a short part of the evening on literacy.

Most parents are eager to help with literacy at home. It helps if we can tell them how they can reinforce some of the teaching we're doing at school. During a parents' evening or a social event arranged to thank parents for their support during the term, offer a session focusing on how the school teaches language. One way of doing this is to show how we model writing and how we help students learn from their mistakes by reassuring them that we all make them. In 'high-stakes' writing, in tests and assessments, we help students by showing them how we cope and develop resilience.

To do this:

- Show parents how one-to-one sessions work.
- Use some extracts from a test that students will have to take. Why a test? It's better to be pragmatic. Parents want to know how students can do well in assessments and examinations. A good example is the GCSE science six-mark question because most students have to answer it and it requires economy of writing. Show some sample questions and exemplar answers.
- Demonstrate how teachers sometimes talk aloud while they write. Show parents how this allows students to see the choices of word, phrase and structure made during writing.

Teaching tip

Show how students are asked to imitate this decision making in their own writing. Show how students are then asked to invent a sentence of their own to practise independence.

IDEA 28

Supporting reluctant writers

'Building students' confidence before the school year starts can make a significant difference to their attitude.'

Some students, often boys, do not respond to traditional writing interventions because they have lost confidence in themselves as writers. You might want to start working with students in June or even May to build their confidence in writing before the school year begins.

Invite students you know to be reluctant writers to a taster session during the summer term where you discuss how they feel about the writing they are asked to do in lessons. Listen without judgement or problem solving. Ask them to bring a piece of writing from any school subject that they are happy to share and ask the group to say what they think is good in each piece. Prompt an extended discussion of content and writing decisions before asking them to write another piece.

Then encourage these students to attend a short series of writing workshops (between six and ten sessions) in which they are asked to write as themselves, not as part of a curriculum task. Set topics for each session, e.g. blame, banter, success, etc.

Word-process the writing they produce between sessions and start the next session by sharing it anonymously and asking for positive feedback from the group. Reward their work publicly with writing certificates and pens.

Taking it further

Ask students who complete all the sessions to nominate another student for the next set of workshops. Successful students can also be asked to mentor students with similar writing issues in the year below them, including accompanying them to a lesson.

IDEA 29

Withdrawal session for disadvantaged students

'This is for anyone leading a student through some literacy work in a withdrawal session.'

This is an example plan for a 30-minute literacy intervention session.

Teaching tip

Follow up in the subject lesson. It helps if a similar structure is offered to the whole class. If it's familiar to the student, it is more likely to become embedded in their repertoire.

In their 2015 report, *Supporting the Attainment of Disadvantaged Students*, the Department for Education found that a withdrawal session is one of a range of interventions that can lead to success. However, their evidence suggests it will be more successful if the withdrawal happens during a non-core lesson rather than taking the student out of the lesson to which the skill applies.

A 30-minute session might look like this:

- This session looks at writing some formal text that might be needed in science.
- Read an exam question. Model how to identify the keywords in the question.
- Plan out the time needed to answer the question. Model how to look at the marks available and the time available.
- Model how to start the answer and how to make six key points using efficient and subject-specific language.
- The student makes an attempt.
- Review the attempt, the modelled version and now, an exemplar answer supplied by the examination board with the student.
- The student makes a second attempt at the same question.

- Now that more marks have been gained, review any features of language that might be applied to other subjects. These commonly include:
  - density of subject-specialist language
  - use of specific words from the question in the answer
  - use of modality (should/could/might/ought)
  - use of cause and effect phrases (this is because/so/therefore/thus)
  - use of comparison phrases (however/this is different from/but)
  - use of active voice (putting the answer at the start of the sentence so that the question is answered early).
- Build a reading activity into the session. Even if it's just ten minutes. Model how an experienced reader settles down for personal reading time. Say out loud how we screen out other distractions. Say what happens when we get started. For example, how we tell ourselves we're going to read at least three pages before doing anything else.
- Read your book while the pupil reads theirs. Then discuss what you have read, what the best part was, what the writer wanted us to feel, imagine or think and whether it worked. These are small steps but regular sharing of reading helps build a lifelong habit.

> **Taking it further**
>
> Repeat the session on a regular and frequent basis, focusing on different subjects. This allows both practice by the student but also helps the student see the transferability across different exam papers.

IDEA 30

Find – Infer – Name – Deduce (FIND)

'FIND is a four-step approach to close reading. At the first step, Find, we pay attention to a text, noticing some of its features.'

By finding easy-to-spot and easy-to-miss features of a text, we look at it closely. It's an activity that all students can get right and it begins to open up a text.

Teaching tip

Consider introducing the other three steps in FIND: **I**nference, **N**aming and **D**eduction. You might be able to find ten minutes in another lesson to focus on reading skills.

As we saw in Idea 12, the first step of the FIND approach to close reading is Find. This focuses on word and letter recognition. It's an activity to remind students how many reading skills they have learned. You choose a passage from a text they're reading in your lesson. Together, you complete activities like these:

- Find any word beginning with a vowel.
- Find a word with a double letter combination.
- Find a word with an unsounded letter.
- Find a subject-specific keyword.
- Find a word similar to a keyword in an examination question.
- Search for a word meaning the opposite of a specific subject keyword.

Done as a whole class and modelled by the teacher, you're making the reading process visible. Include advice on what to do when you're stuck, so you're reminding students what they can do.

Taking it further

Have students write a short passage about which they devise similar questions for a partner to answer.

What we are doing here is building up students' confidence. Too many students think they can't read well enough to do well in tests and examinations. We need to show them the skills they have.

IDEA 31

The full stop in five minutes

'You're teaching literacy if you spend just five minutes describing the full stop.'

You don't have much time. You're focusing on the content of your subject. Yet you want to help the students focus on their literacy. This is the first step in a three-step approach called describe – show – practise and it will help you teach the full stop in five minutes.

You only have five minutes, so it's better to be direct. Keep your teaching of the full stop simple and straightforward and use a whole-class approach so that no one is left behind. Support the whole-class teaching with individual support in normal circulation round the class.

Describe: tell students what the full stop does. Use definitions they are familiar with:

- It helps the reader take a breath.
- It organises information.
- It separates ideas.
- It tells examiners you've made a key point.

Teaching tip

Have students read their work to each other, speaking out loud the punctuation marks as they reach them. This is a quick reminder of their importance and it allows you to check their use.

Taking it further

You might want to do something a little memorable like having student volunteers play, in role, a conversation a full stop might have with you. Model it first. You might be in role as a full stop, explaining how important you are for creating ideas and how you don't like being absent. Just this activity helps students notice and pay attention to their literacy.

IDEA 32

The full stop in ten minutes

'This is a useful three-step process to warming up a literacy skill.'

Describe – show – practise is a three-step approach that enables everyone to see how the full stop works. Get students to experience getting it right before they start.

> **Teaching tip**
>
> Some writers refer to the 'three line rule'. This anecdotal guide reminds writers in test conditions that very few sentences go on longer than three lines without a full stop.

You may only have five to ten minutes, so, as in Idea 31, it's better to be direct. Keep your teaching of the full stop simple and straightforward and use a whole-class approach so that no one is left behind. Support the whole-class teaching with individual support in normal circulation round the class.

Try these three steps:

- **Describe:** tell students what the full stop does. Use definitions they are familiar with: it helps the reader take a breath; it organises information; it separates ideas; it tells examiners you've made a key point.
- **Show:** show some examples from the text the students are reading in your class. Show it with and without full stops.
- **Practise:** you talk out loud as you practise writing a full stop. Choose a sentence similar to the type of writing to be used in the lesson. Then students have a go so that everyone gets it right.

IDEA 33

The full stop in over ten minutes

'These additional steps to the describe – show – practise approach really deepen students' learning.'

Following the structure describe – show – practise – independence – application when teaching the full stop enables students to come at the skill from lots of different angles. That's what's important, not remembering a specific order of steps.

Helping students see the point of punctuation is often successful if more than one teacher does it. Very few teachers of subjects other than English have the time to give it the sort of close attention explained here. So if you do, students will notice it and make a vital connection to their English lessons. Even if you only do this once a term, you're probably adding significantly to their provision.

The first three steps of this activity (describe – show – practise) are the same as in Idea 32. After completing these steps, add two more layers of practice:

- **Independence:** students complete the 'practise' step for a partner. Check accuracy and reward success. They model for their partner what they do when they use a full stop, explaining it and showing it. If students haven't got it, get them to have another go and support this in circulation time.
- **Application:** now students get into the lesson content. Students write two or three sentences in response to the task you've set to help learn the subject. You check this in circulation and students make corrections quickly.

Taking it further

Have the students choose a couple of pages anywhere in their exercise books. They go back over it and rewrite a short section including any missing full stops. By doing this, they're combining review of content with accuracy of punctuation. In a following week, have students set each other a simple cloze exercise using two sentences from their own writing. They miss out the full stop and have their partner place it correctly.

IDEA 34

Writing about subject knowledge

'This is a great warm-up practice if you've got ten to 15 minutes before students start extended writing.'

If students are to gain the highest marks, they need to explain knowledge in some detail. This activity shows more able students how to use a range of vocabulary about subject content.

Teaching tip

Give students an attempt at the **imagine – imitate – innovate** structure. Here, students are shown a piece of writing and asked to imagine who wrote it, when and why. Then they imitate it using as many grammatical words as they like from the source. Finally, they write a six-minute imitation of the text and share it with peers for comparison with the original.

Taking it further

Publish the writing scoring the highest marks in the students' books. This is less frequently done but it can help some students to have examples in their books of high-quality writing by their peers.

Use the T cards in the online resources (see Idea 68) and an image such as the one also included in the online resources to help with this activity.

- Show the students an image that makes them think or that provokes curiosity.
- Discuss what the image makes students imagine, feel, think or do.
- Infer the image maker's intention. You model trying to use five or six of the words from the 'Know' playing card (see the T cards in the online resources).
- Students have a time deadline to write their answer on the card using all the words.
- Discuss what the students have done using the visualiser. Explain which writing would have secured the higher marks according to the subject-specific grade criteria. Explain which words proved more helpful.

IDEA 35

Writing about understanding

'This activity helps students develop their thinking literacy. It's a practice that can be used before extended writing in any subject.'

If students are to gain the highest marks, they may need to show understanding or explain their 'working out'. Paying close attention to the vocabulary of understanding can help more able students to do this.

Use the T cards (see Idea 68), T scripts and image in the online resources to help with this activity.

- Show the students the image in the online resources.
- Discuss what it makes you imagine, feel, think or do.
- Infer the image maker's intention.
- Students challenge the teacher to model using all the words on the 'Understanding' T card. Some students find it helpful to see the teacher trying to do this.
- You might want to use the T script resource. It's a challenge because the vocabulary is more extensive and not all of it will be familiar.
- Students write what they understand and don't understand about the image. It might help to pair students up. Assign each writer a reader partner.
- Have a pair of students explain to the class the strengths of their partner's writing. Link this to an examination question. Tell students which words from the card would help get the highest marks.

Teaching tip

Students might be shown a piece of writing that would score a high mark. They highlight all the grammatical words. They are allowed to use any of these in their writing. This draws their attention to adverbial phrases, conjunctions and clause structures used by a successful writer.

Taking it further

Publish the best writing in an online anthology of successful examination practices. Students may find it helpful when they know the students who wrote revision exemplars.

IDEA 36

Punctuation challenge

'This is a quick activity for any teacher to focus attention on punctuation. It's just another way of reminding students to check for accuracy.'

This is a five-minute excursion into the importance of punctuation. It can be set to a group of the most able students or most confident language users. They prepare the response as an extension.

- Have students remove all the punctuation from a short piece of text.
- They present the piece to the class and have the class decide which are the three most important pieces of punctuation to be replaced.
- The students then explain to the class where punctuation came from. Challenge them to look up the history of several punctuation marks and when they first appeared in writing.
- Finally, you could have the students in role as the replaced punctuation. They make a case for why they are the single most important mark.

Taking it further

As part of a homework response, students could be asked to explain one punctuation mark they've used. This is easy to do if they choose the full stop, so challenge students to write a sentence about the comma, which is frequently overlooked and often ignored altogether.

IDEA 37

Experimenting with prepositions

'This is for any subject teacher wanting to challenge their most able students.'

Using a variety of prepositions extends students' language repertoire. With frequent practice, students will become more skilled at choosing the right word to make the point they need in exam or classroom writing.

Use the preposition list in the online resources – this is a list of 48 of the most commonly used prepositions, which is easily enough for a different one for each member of the class.

Give one preposition to each member of the class and try the following activities in pairs:

- In four lines (two each) and using the preposition you've been given:
  - *Describe to a witness that you've just seen a UFO.*
  - *Tell your partner something about the lesson you've just had.*
  - *Describe what you want to do with the A levels you're going to take in post-16 learning.*

The point of limiting the number of lines is to enable you to get on with the lesson quickly. Students are also likely to want another go, or to have more lines to say. Tell them that their chance will come in the writing you're going to do in the lesson. The point of the practice is to help learn the content in your lesson. If you do have time for more, have students exchange their preposition once or twice in two different role plays.

Teaching tip

Have pupils see when the prepositions have been used in exemplar examination board answers. Prepositions are helpful when trying to establish cause and effect, link events by time and make an argument or clarify an explanation.

Taking it further

Have students create model answers for the school's literacy library. Create lists of sentences that use each of the 48 most commonly used prepositions. The idea is to help other students see the point of having a range of prepositions available to you.

Developing student leaders

Part 5

IDEA 38

The emotional literacy leader

'This activity helps students learn how to encourage the language of resilience and leadership. Students lead by noticing the ways their peers are being considerate, thoughtful and cooperative.'

Leaders encourage positive language about emotions and attitudes. Teach students how to lead in this way by putting them in charge of noticing inclusive, resilient talk and listening.

This activity can be used in tutor time or in class to help students develop their leadership skills.

- Put an emotional literacy leader card (see online resources) face down on two students' places before they come into the classroom. It helps to brief students beforehand. Let students know this is a reward for their observational, leadership or language skills.
- The card says: *You are part of a team noticing emotional literacy. Think of words and phrases that might describe the emotions you think have helped learning today. You're noticing emotions rather than students.*
- This leadership role is best done from where the students sit. They might write their observations just for the teacher to read at first.
- The kinds of language we might want to promote are those that encourage resilience. So, ask students to notice:
  - confidence when starting new or challenging work
  - willingness to learn from mistakes
  - cooperation between students
  - consideration of others' needs
  - politeness and turn-taking
  - a willingness to share with others ways of completing a task.
- When students grow in skill, they are able to share with the class what they've observed.

Teaching tip

There is a range of helpful resources about the way emotions are handled in schools. You might like to look at the work being done at the Oxford Mindfulness Centre: **www.oxfordmindfulness.org**

Taking it further

Students might use a thesaurus to grow their vocabulary around emotions that have been noticed. They might also think of attitudes that would help if they were encouraged by their peers. Letting parents know that students have taken on this responsibility can help reinforce the confidence of these leaders.

IDEA 39

The greeter

'Teach students the language of politeness, courtesy and learning.'

This can be a useful activity for helping students learn the language of politeness, courtesy and learning. Used occasionally it improves curiosity about the learning in the classroom. It also helps improve behaviour and attitudes to learning.

Choose one or two of your students to be the class greeter(s). This helps build their speaking skills, especially when you model for them modes of address and how to talk about learning.

Put the greeter card (see online resources) on the chosen students' places. The instructions on the card read as follows:

You are leading the welcome to a class visitor. It helps if you stand up and use any of the following phrases when the visitor enters:

- 'Good morning/afternoon.'
- 'Welcome to our class.'
- 'How can we help you?'

You're making the lesson important. You're giving status to the visit. It takes about two minutes. You'll create a memory that will last at least the rest of the day.

After greeting the visitor as instructed, the student might ask the visitor, 'Can I tell you what we're learning today?' This can help reinforce the learning objectives. The visitor almost always says yes to this. The greeter reads the learning objectives from their book or the board. The rest of the class is given a reminder of the purpose of the lesson.

Taking it further

The greeter might close by saying something positive about the class, such as, 'This is the hardest working class in Year 11.' So, in these few moments, the greeter has reinforced the lesson, demonstrated politeness and courtesy and affirmed the class. Formal interpersonal language has been used, for a purpose, to an audience.

IDEA 40

The chair leader

'Being a chairperson can help a student to focus on a range of sentence types and encourages turn-taking.'

This activity helps any subject or form teacher develop their students' skills in organised discussions.

Asking a student to be a chairperson teaches them the language skills of summing up, concluding, asking questions to deepen the discussion, turn-taking and encouraging politeness. It can also be helpful for teaching the four types of sentence in English: command, statement, question and exclamation. To teach these skills, we could provide a variety of possible phrases, sentence types and question starters. We need to model their use and help the chair leaders and the class.

To nominate chair leaders, place four chairperson cards (see online resources) on the desks of the students you want to learn these skills. The cards have the following instructions:

> You are the chairperson for today. There might be times in the lesson when we will be discussing as a whole group or small groups. You will be leading the discussions.
> You might find it useful to move between four types of sentence: command, statement, question and exclamation.
> You will learn how to help turn-taking, timekeeping, thinking time and helping the group learn skills and knowledge.

Whenever you wish, you set up a discussion activity and invite the chair leaders to take a lead role. Chair leaders might work together, chairing a whole-class discussion as a group. Alternatively, the class might be divided into four groups with one of the chairs leading each of the groups.

Teaching tip

You should model for the chair leaders how to start, encourage questions and sum up, how to include everyone, encourage different views and keep on focus. You could ask the chair leaders to give feedback on their work. Ask them to focus on the language. Ask them to report phrases that seemed to help turn-taking, deepen thinking or allow thinking time.

What you're doing is offering a little more structure to language learning. You are raising the profile of language phrases that might help learning. So, you might encourage modal phrases like:

- I wonder if...
- The reason could be...
- Might this be because...
- Should it be this way...?

And question starters like:

- What if...?
- Why might that be...?
- How many causes are there?

Chair leaders might also find it helpful to ask questions that invite peers to think of a variety of outcomes and responses.

> **Taking it further**
>
> You could focus for several lessons on one chair skill more than any other. For example, the chair leader might encourage thinking time. So, with the class, develop a phrase that does this. For example, 'When you hear the chair leader say, "Don't answer straight away", this means we are taking a few moments to think through an answer before we speak.'

IDEA 41

The learning to learn leader

'This activity helps listening and encourages quality talk about learning. It's for any class teacher.'

You might ask some students to be 'learning to learn' leaders. These students help others use quality speaking and listening skills. You can vary the students taking up these roles during the term.

Teaching tip

It is sometimes more effective if the four learning to learn leaders work together as a group, rather than individually.

Put a learning to learn leader card (see online resources) face down on four students' places before they come into class.

When students reach their place and see they are learning to learn leader, they read on the card their job and responsibilities. For example:

You are the learning to learn leader.

When instructed, you will go round the class and look for signs of [for example, thinking, wondering, helping each other, asking questions, making corrections and learning from mistakes.]

The teacher decides when the leaders can go round the classroom. The teacher tells the students what to look for. This depends on the lesson; there's no absolute skill set. Some examples are given above, and on the opposite page.

The leaders share with the class what learning seemed to be effective. This might be part of the mid-lesson plenary so there's time to build on what's been discovered.

Examples of what you might ask your learning to learn leaders to look for include:

- listening to each other
- good turn-taking
- questioning each other and the teacher with open and closed questions, showing signs of curiosity
- using modal verb constructions – *could be/might be/should make/would create* – showing they are wondering about outcomes or creating the conditions for unexpected outcomes and so planning steps of learning
- using language of evaluation: *there are reasons why; the strength of this is; the weaknesses are; this has value in the market because; this could be improved if ...*
- have the learning to learn leader put the word 'learn' into the online thesaurus for all to see. Then choose the most fitting words for this lesson: 'Have we done more than remembered? Have we understood or compared or synthesized or created?'
- ask the learning to learn leader to teach the others phrases for building up ideas in a longer answer. These might include: on the other hand; this is just like; it is as if; this suggests; however. Next, the learning to learn leader should have the class work in groups of five. They invent a paragraph about the learning topic using all five of these phrases.

> **Bonus idea** ★
>
> Students discuss the market place value of talking and writing about learning. They might consider how, in product evaluation meetings, for example, some businesses use the principles of 'kaizen' (show students the Japanese character; see online resources). This is a means by which groups of producers engage in discussion about improvement on a regular and systematic basis. (It's been most notably employed by Toyota in their product development.)

IDEA 42

The literacy coordinator

'This can be a game changer in your literacy teaching.'

You might nominate a student to be your literacy coordinator for the week, month or term. Choose one, two or three students. Change the roles so perhaps half the class have had the job by the end of the year.

This is one of a variety of possible student plenary leaders. It encourages high-quality speaking and also reinforces the emphasis on the importance of language skills in every lesson. Try offering the roles irregularly and infrequently. Why? Building in an element of surprise helps sustain interest in the process.

Put a literacy coordinator card (see online resources) face down on three students' places before the students come into class. When students reach their place and see they are literacy coordinator, they have the following rights and responsibilities:

- Students decide, in discussion with the teacher, what counts as high-quality language in this lesson.
- At particular points in the lesson, you instruct the literacy coordinators to go round the classroom to look for instances of this high-quality language in students' discussions or written work.
- Students report to the class what they have seen, read or heard and why it is high quality. They could demonstrate some of this on the class visualiser.

Teaching tip

Students might be given the responsibility to choose when they go round the classroom. When they get used to the role, students become skilled at knowing when would be appropriate and helpful times to lead.

Taking it further

Students discuss the uses of leadership language used by the literacy coordinators. Phrases that suggest politeness, encouragement and support are reinforced.

Part 6

Training staff and promoting literacy in staff meetings

IDEA 43

Literacy is a shared responsibility

'This is a quick activity to open up discussions about literacy among staff.'

Staff meeting time is short, so here's something that takes 15 to 20 minutes to engage all staff in discussions about the importance of literacy in your school.

Drawing from evidence, you can suggest to staff that the language policy will be effective if based on:

- what we all need in this school
- what's needed at this time
- what we know about the current cohort of students.

Distribute the three cards in the online resources. They are extracts from Ofsted's report, *Improving Literacy in Secondary Schools: A Shared Responsibility* (April, 2013).

Have staff read the cards in subject teams and work on the following:

- Card 1: How true is this at our school? What are the implications for improving literacy?
- Card 2: What are the top three skills students in my subject need?
- Card 3: What should the whole school emphasis be?

Ask staff to record their responses on A1 sheets. Collect them in and pin them up round the staffroom. It's a simple visual representation of the school's language focus.

Taking it further

Photograph each A1 sheet, scan them to PDF and put them in your policy. The benefit of this is ownership. If the first pages of the policy are a reminder of the shared thinking the staff did, it's more likely the policy will be seen as 'ours' and less of an imposition.

IDEA 44

Team approach to spelling

'This simple suggestion to your department, your year group team or even your whole staff can have significant and far-reaching effects.'

You may find that too many misspellings are going uncorrected or the same spelling mistakes are being repeated. Give staff the opportunity to share techniques for improving spelling. They are more likely use approaches that make sense to them rather than those imposed.

A simple, 20-minute session with your staff might help improve spelling across your school. Show some examples of work from books and get staff to say how they've managed spelling corrections. There is no right way but staff will want to see what's worked in their school. This may include:

- Students have been set regular quizzes on words they have been getting wrong.
- Students are required to copy out the correct spellings of three words as part of their corrections.
- Staff set regular spelling tests on words they must know to get high marks in their subject.

By keeping your approach simple, there is a much greater chance that something will happen. By allowing staff to use approaches that are already working for students in their school, there's more chance of adoption.

Teaching tip

You might invite some students to the staff training session. Ask them to share with staff what helps them get spellings right. With their agreement, have them show examples from their books.

Taking it further

Build a spelling section on the school website with department tabs so that, within a few clicks, students and parents can get to subject-specific word lists. It's something parents and students can use to set spelling tests or quizzes for themselves at home. Parents often appreciate being able to do something clear and specific.

IDEA 45

Student literacy presentations

'Why not have students tell your department team what's working for them in literacy learning?'

You might find teaching literacy even more effective by having students talk with the subject team about what helps them learn.

Once a year, prepare a group of students to give a 15-minute presentation to all staff in a department. Students can be from any group or year group, but it can help the students if there is a mix of ability, group and age.

Invite students to share with the subject team short presentations about language. Set the preparation as a piece of homework. Get students to practise for five minutes as a homework plenary. When they present, if you can, offer them a visualiser so they can display some of their work.

The students could discuss:

- favourite books they are reading, have read or want to read
- extracts from their writing that make them proud
- spelling activities that have helped
- pieces of marked work and what they have done as follow-up
- extended writing examples and how it's helped them understand subject knowledge
- how they have remembered key subject-specific terms
- revision techniques they have found to work
- lesson activities that have really helped
- best beginnings and endings to lessons
- the most interesting homework activities
- how the class libraries could be even better.

Teaching tip

The presentation might link directly to the subject team's planning focus. You might find this particularly helpful if you know there are strong outcomes in some classes, as you can share these colleagues' practice.

Bonus idea ★

Students set written work for the staff to do, which they then mark. They should be short 'curiosity pieces' about aspects of the subject that make them curious. What we're doing is promoting the subject, using reading, and writing for real audiences.

IDEA 46

A homework plan is a literacy plan

'You'll be surprised how much literacy is already being offered.'

If you're a head of year and you want to plan a literacy programme for your students, take a look at their homework planners. Everything they are set from right across the curriculum will be literacy based.

Sometimes you might be able to map the extended writing being taught to students as homework tasks. You might therefore already have a homework plan that could be adapted to become an extended literacy grid. To do this:

- Ask each subject team what written work they are going to set over the course of a term as homework.
- Present these plans to students, teachers and their parents so they can make links between subject areas.
- Parents can track what their children are doing and offer whatever support is helpful.
- By the end of term, you can gauge the progress of students by comparing the early attempts with the latest.
- You can publish the work on the school's website for students to see the wide range of styles and techniques adopted by their peers.
- This could also become a library of reading resources for teachers. You can suggest to colleagues that students might use these texts to practise their inference or close reading skills and even use them as examination practices.
- Many students find it motivating to read material they know has been written by their peers.

Taking it further

Each department might suggest a second piece of homework that is written for an audience outside the school. It can be highly motivating for students to know that their work might be read by real readers.

IDEA 47

Research extracts

'This staff training activity helps create a sense that the school's literacy policy is owned by the whole team.'

In a training session, you might want to share with your staff some selected extracts from research around what makes effective literacy teaching. This gives staff the opportunity to contribute to the improvement of the schools' literacy policy.

In the online resources, you will find a range of extracts from relevant research in the field. They are from reasonably well-known sources, such as the Department for Education, Ofsted, UKRA, The Institute of Education (University of London) and The Sutton Trust to address the credibility issue. The research extracts are in group sets, each tackling a different aspect of literacy planning and implementation.

First, create home groups. These might be subject team groups. The home groups have a go at the following questions:

- Read each research extract in their set, perhaps in pairs to begin with.
- What implications does this have for our subject team?

Next, redivide colleagues into rainbow groups. Number each member of the home group one to six. All of the ones, twos and so on regroup. These are the rainbow groups. Each member of the rainbow group will have been looking at a different set of research extracts, so ask each member to do the following:

- Give one piece of new knowledge to your group.
- Discuss the implication for your school.

Teaching tip

It's so useful to keep the literacy policy alive by adding to it with practical ideas that colleagues have found work. Suggest to department teams that once a term they add an idea they are trying. Try and keep alive the sense that the work they are doing together is collective school research. You might also invite the school council to contribute ideas to your research. This might be in two forms: literacy support they want and teaching ideas they've experienced that have helped.

You'll need about 15 minutes to do this.

Finally, reconvene the home group. Each member has now acquired a set of new thinking from their rainbow group. So, allow them another 15 minutes to discuss the following:

- What do you recommend we do:
  - in the short term (the next 6 weeks)
  - the medium term (the next term)
  - and the long term (the next six months)?

Taking it further

Home groups can put their ideas onto a sheet of A1. You pin these up around the room and invite the groups to see what others have written. You could make a photo record of each A1 sheet. These, reformatted as PDFs, make a useful inclusion in the school's literacy policy. It's a record of the project's journey, a commitment to the school-specific nature of the policy and a demonstration of policy ownership by the whole team.

IDEA 48

Planning grid

'Try using a planning grid to design your plans for literacy across the curriculum.'

There is no right way to plan. The best approach is the one that suits you and your school. However, an effective planning grid is always a good place to start.

You'll find an example planning grid in the online resources. Here's how to use it:

- In the first column, list the subjects you want to focus on. (You might list year groups or student groups instead. Remember, the grid is a suggested approach.)
- There's also a line for a whole-school focus. Keep these manageable. The more you have, the more difficult it will be to manage. Try to select a focus that will make the greatest difference to the most students in the shortest time.
- The second column is for outcomes. There are things students might do, skills they might learn and measurements we might use.
- The other columns are for planning literacy activities to help achieve these outcomes.

Let's take an example:

- Suppose we decide to work with the geography team. It might be that your book scrutiny has shown students have readily identifiable literacy skills needs in geography.
- Your focus on geography might be because you get on well with the head of geography. Forming alliances with colleagues can be a critically important part of the process and there are always groups in any subject area who would benefit from a focused intervention.

Teaching tip

You'll also see that I've included a chance to agree possible audiences for any writing or reading outcome. There are two audiences included as examples: audiences in school and out of school (don't forget to discuss this with the school's designated safeguarding lead).

- Agree the priority student groups, the literacy focus, the skills to be taught and the writing or reading outcomes. In practice, agreeing these things can take a term. Do not be dismayed; this is perfectly normal! If you've found time for a discussion with a subject leader, you're doing well.
- Take about 30 minutes or so to look at a few books from the focus group. Notice features that the head of geography needs. Spelling, handwriting and use of specialist vocabulary may well feature strongly.
- Agree an approach. The head of geography will have colleagues at various stages of experience. To achieve a consistent approach, it'll have to be quickly and easily understood.
- So, for example, suggest the head of geography's colleagues try the following: teach students to regularly correct their own work. It's an essential examination and life skill. Here's how you might recommend this is done:
  - In one marking cycle, colleagues might require students to write out the corrected versions of three spelling errors.
  - In the next marking cycle, colleagues require students to rewrite a sentence that needs to be more legible.
  - In the third cycle, as part of their response to marking, students are required to write a sentence with a specialist term used correctly.

Taking it further

What if this became a routine? It will if colleagues can see results. They will need to be encouraged to build students' patience. It may take a term. Colleagues have many other features to develop in their students' understanding. Be encouraged that, if this becomes a learning habit, significant progress may be made. The key to the success of any approach to language development is to make it manageable and consistent. You will be the best judge. Introducing any change to the practice of colleagues requires them to see the sense of it and have some ownership.

Part 7

Lessons – all subject areas

IDEA 49

2–3–4

'This is a really effective and quick literacy idea for building students' speaking and listening skills.'

This simple routine can help build pace and bring focus to learning through oracy. It works to reinforce content, build curiosity and helps you assess what students understand and what they may need a little extra help with.

This activity can be used at the start, in the middle or at the end of any lesson. First, teach the class what it means. Say, 'When I say 2–3–4, you have **two** minutes to tell **three** people **four** things you learned last lesson.'

You can vary the numbers to suit the level of challenge you want. You can also vary the task from 'things you learned' to 'things you want to know', 'keywords in our subject', 'questions about the topic', or 'ideas for developing the project further'.

Taking it further

You may get to a point where you simply introduce the theme, e.g. 'things you want to know,' and then a number sequence, setting the students off in the routine. It can become an efficient process for getting learning happening quickly and with minimum exposition. You can walk into class and say something like, 'Good morning. Questions we haven't asked yet. Ready? 2–2–2. Let's go.'

IDEA 50

Description warm-up

'Students need to describe processes, events, causes and features in a range of subjects.'

This is a warm-up activity that you'll find useful for helping students describe processes and objects effectively.

Promote curiosity by challenging students to describe anything they see. The trick is not to tell anyone what is being described until partners have had a go at guessing what it is. Here's how:

- Students notice a part of the room but keep it to themselves.
- They describe the object or place to a partner without telling them where it is; their partner tries to guess what they are describing.
- Students say what they were thinking of if their partner does not guess correctly.
- Have students describe another object but this time, describe it from the point of view of the object itself. If they want, students can imagine the feelings this object might have. It might start like this:

    'I wish people would notice me. If you look closely, there's more to me than meets the eye.'

- This works well if students choose something in the room that is often overlooked, such as the paint on the wall, the clock, the fire extinguisher or a whiteboard pen.
- The point is to promote curiosity in the audience. The key is to get students thinking about having an effect on the audience.

> **Bonus idea** ★
>
> Take the class on a walk around the school and ask them to look for signs of change. Students are often surprised by how everything is influenced by interrelationships. Have students choose places that have been affected by what people have done or what's been influenced by natural forces. Ask students to describe the changes they notice.

IDEA 51

Three tokens

'I find it helpful every so often to play this game to remind students how important listening is.'

This quick game encourages close listening and turn-taking. Students find it reassuring to know that even if they aren't contributing with ideas or questions, they can still be working and learning.

Teaching tip

Explain to students that the tokens represent both the *right* to speak and also the *responsibility* to speak.

In a group discussion, each student is given three tokens (these can be lollipop sticks, beans, etc.). Each time they speak they 'spend' one token. When they have used all their tokens and have none left to spend, they cannot speak and need simply to listen.

What happens is that students think carefully about when they're going to spend their tokens. They listen to what's being said and judge when their contribution will be most helpful. They will pause, think and weigh up the value of speaking if they know that these opportunities to speak are limited to three. Others who might have remained silent throughout have a tangible reminder in their hand that they, like everyone else, have things to contribute.

When you next do some speaking work, remind students of this game and ask them to think of the tokens they used here.

IDEA 52

Listening with the whole self

'I found this to be quite a game changer. When we shared the image around the school and with parents, it became the default definition of good-quality listening. It helped that a few students were able to pronounce it. They became real stars in the school community.'

This idea is useful in form time or in any subject lesson. It involves discussing with the class what the traditional Chinese character for listening denotes.

The traditional Chinese character for listening is:

聴

A definition is as follows:

- The section on the top left denotes the '**ear**'. The bottom left section denotes the '**mind**'.
- There are four sections on the right. The top one denotes '**you**'. Beneath that is a symbol for the **eyes**. Next is '**undivided attention**'.
- The final part, supporting the rest is '**heart**'.

At first, show students the character without comment (an enlarged version is available in the online resources). Some students might know it. If they don't, suggest some clues. Ask students what they think are the three most important skills to listening. Accept whatever is useful, then offer the definition above.

Discuss what it means to listen with your ear, yourself, your eyes and your heart. Discuss what undivided attention means.

Teaching tip

Check whether there is a school description of high-quality listening. If there isn't, ask students to think about what it might be. Would it differ depending on the context, e.g. the classroom, the library, the dinner hall or the corridor?

IDEA 53

Mnemonics

'This is a surprisingly underused technique. For many students, mnemonics work well, especially when you get them to make up their own and they link with features of the school, the local area or the classroom.'

Some students find that making and using mnemonics helps them notice the spelling of keywords and they are especially useful in examinations.

There are a number of ways in which mnemonics can be used:

- Some help students remember specific subject content, e.g.
  No **P**lan **L**ike **Y**ours **T**o **S**tudy **H**istory **W**isely
  (Norman, Plantagenet, Lancaster, York, Tudor, Stuart, Hanover, Windsor)
- Some help students remember specific word groups, e.g. the essential amino acids:
  Pvt. Tim Hall
  (Phenylalanine, Valine, Threonine, Tryptophan, Isoleucine, Methionine, Histidine, Arginine, Leucine, Lysine)
- Some help students spell difficult words, e.g.
  Rhythm **H**elps **Y**our **T**wo **H**ips **M**ove (RHYTHM).

Have your students come up with a mnemonic relevant to your subject. They can generate the mnemonics with a thesaurus. First, explain to students what the mnemonic should represent and instruct them to take each letter in turn. Model finding a word to represent the first item or letter, offering alternatives by displaying your word in a synonym list in the thesaurus. Ask the class to find as many words as they need to build their individual mnemonics.

Taking it further

Have another class test out the mnemonics by using them in their work. Invite the other class to give two-paragraph responses to the mnemonic. Paragraph one: what they liked about the mnemonic. Paragraph two: either a mnemonic of their own or suggestions for changing the mnemonic. The important thing here is to get students to use the key vocabulary, to talk about the words, to arrange them and rearrange them, and to notice them and their spelling.

Bonus idea ★

Take your class into the room they'll take their examinations in. Then ask students to build mnemonics based on what they can see in the room.

IDEA 54

Cloze activity for keywords

'Getting students to devise teaching materials for each other can help them learn spellings and punctuation rules.'

Some students find it helpful when they think about how keywords fit grammatically into a sentence. Asking students to create cloze activities for peers to complete can help them to do this.

This activity involves having students devise a cloze activity for a partner to complete. Here's how:

- Choose the same keyword for all students. This is a term or knowledge word essential for the lesson, test or examination.
- Model its use in role play with a volunteer. Say, for example, 'When plants engage in **photosynthesis**, oxygen is produced and carbon dioxide is absorbed.' Then repeat the sentence 'hiding' any of the keywords. The volunteer has to remember what you said. Just say the word 'blank' for 'photosynthesis'.
- Now set students the challenge of devising a cloze activity by writing a short text with at least four keywords hidden. Their partner completes it. It's as simple as that. The clear, stepped structure is what helps students secure the keywords.

Taking it further

Try the reverse. Supply three cards each with a keyword written on them. Students place the cards on their exercise books. They leave spaces where words might go to complete a sentence using these keywords. Their partner writes in the spaces what they think is missing. It doesn't matter if they match what their partner first thought of. The point is using the keywords accurately.

IDEA 55

Look, say, cover, write, check, use

'For lots of students, this is the default method of learning a new spelling. They don't have to do all the steps all the time, but knowing there's a system they can turn to helps students feel secure with new and complicated spellings.'

This technique helps students learn the spelling of a word. Some students just use two elements of the process, those which they know help them, but the idea is to develop a routine that the student knows works for them. Learning spelling is more helpful to most students when they compete with themselves rather than others.

Teaching tip

At parents' evening, parents will often ask what they can do to help their children with spelling. Why not teach them this approach?

Many students need a degree of focus on a new word, especially if they've got it wrong frequently or it's unfamiliar. Teach students the entirety of the following process for learning a new spelling and they can use the steps that work best for them each time they come across a new word:

- **Look:** Ask the students to look at the words. See if they can find patterns, words within words, repeated letters, letters of their own name, letters of a sports team and how the word begins and ends.
- **Say:** Suggest the students say the word slowly or as quickly as they can, whisper it, chant it or sing it.
- **Cover:** Just for a second. Or longer if you want the students to challenge one another. What's the longest time they can cover it and still remember it?
- **Write:** Tell the students to write the word in the same pen as they normally use or would use in an examination. Or, perhaps they could use the largest pen they have. Or write the word so it's barely detectable, as large as the page will allow or with each letter very

securely separated. Or in capitals. Or with shading. Perhaps as a town welcome sign, a billboard or part of road map.
- **Check:** The students look back and congratulate themselves for any part they got right.
- **Use:** The more memorable the sentence the better. But keep it simple at first: instruct students to write it in an accurate subject-specific context. Then, perhaps, try it as an alliteration, or a rhyming couplet, or a paradox.

Taking it further

Be the words.
Adventurous students may be helped by 'becoming' the word for a moment and introducing themselves to a partner. As part of the introduction, they may want to tell their partner their history. Some find it helps if they've seen or done some basic etymology.

IDEA 56

The inventor of words

'Getting students to think about words as inventions makes them think about their origins, history and spelling.'

Sometimes, students don't spell a word accurately because they don't look at it closely enough. This exercise can help when introducing new vocabulary. It involves the class 'inventing' the word they need to spell.

Some students find their language develops through being made curious. In this exercise, we see existing words as if we'd invented them. You can even make up words to describe emotions, colours or new technology.

There are two ways of doing this:

1. Ask students to imagine that you invented the specialist vocabulary of the lesson. You are an 'inventor of words'. Students then test you about the words as if you invented them. For example, 'Where were you when you came up with the word?' or 'What happened to make you invent it?' or 'Why that word and not another?' Ask the students to test your knowledge of the words. Invite them to ask you the most difficult questions they can. If they are stuck, ask them to spend two minutes in pairs, using 'wh' question words. Before you write the word, offer students the chance to test your spelling of the words.

2. Have students talk to each other about a new word they have found relating to the lesson content. How did they discover it, what uses might it have and why is it spelled that way? Students reply as if they are experts. You're making the word memorable by spending time with it and using it in play.

Taking it further

If you can, challenge students to find out where the words actually came from. A little *real* knowledge of the history of a word can help students' spelling and interest.

IDEA 57

Word continuum

'This helps students play with words and think through the effect of making word choices. Students need to know how important it is to be intentional about choosing the vocabulary of their writing.'

You may want to use this activity to challenge students to consider the nuances between word meaning. This can help students grow their vocabulary. So, for example, in examinations, students will be able to write about effects in more detail.

- Choose a word students might use to describe the effect of a force, a colour, a fabric or whatever links to the lesson content.
- Demonstrate the online thesaurus. Put the word into the search field and see what comes up. Say you've put in the word 'soft'. Up comes: 'squashy', 'spongy', 'supple', 'pliable', 'elastic'.
- Five students each write one of these alternative words on a whiteboard. They sit in a line facing the class.
- Another student puts 'soft' on their whiteboard. They sit in front of the line.
- Now ask the student with 'squashy' to sit next to the student with the 'soft' whiteboard. Ask the class how close in meaning they are. If they think they are very close, they stay sat next to each other. Distance indicates distance in meaning. If words overlap in meaning, have the students sit slightly behind.
- There will be debate and that's what you're after. The point is that there should be differences in interpretation. We are helping students to see there is a wide range of possibilities when writing an explanation.

Teaching tip

Have students use the thesaurus tool to gather words similar to key adjectives used in their subject area. Students can gather these key adjectives from examples of high-grade written work.

Taking it further

Have students read through a piece of work in their exercise books. For homework, ask them to find synonyms for the words they originally chose using the online thesaurus and list them at the end of the piece of writing. It can make a change for students instead of or in addition to correcting their spellings.

IDEA 58

Modelling the online thesaurus

'It's surprising how little students use an online thesaurus. It's also surprising how little they see it used in lessons. It's one of the most time-efficient ways for teachers to develop vocabulary.'

Something as simple and easy as modelling how to use an online thesaurus encourages experimentation and develops vocabulary growth. The key is little and often.

Try making an online thesaurus or the thesaurus in Microsoft Word a regular part of your lessons for two or three weeks. Use it as part of how you model writing exam answers. When you reach a word, for example, that describes a process or an effect, invite alternatives from the students. Then access the thesaurus on the classroom screen. This shows the students how easy it is. Discuss the benefits of the different word options. Make a selection and discuss the impact on marks scored in the answer.

Have students do the same and discuss in pairs the different choices available and their effect. Having students test out alternative word choices in discussion can help secure confidence before writing.

Doing this with frequency and regularity can help students expand their vocabulary. You might even agree as a staff the most effective thesaurus for your students and create a link to this on your school website for students and families.

> **Teaching tip**
>
> You might embed on your staff laptop a shortcut to an online thesaurus. This will mean you can quickly access it whenever you want to discuss word choice with your class.

IDEA 59

Build a thought

'This activity is for any class teacher. It helps students put together their thinking as they write.'

In this technique, a writer or speaker repeats a word or expression while adding more detail to it. In explanation, persuasion and opinion writing, this can help to add emphasis to reinforce a point, a claim or a belief.

Explain the importance of experimentation to your students. Tell them that in crafting language effects, success is rarely achieved the first, second or third time. If you can, try modelling an attempt to have an effect yourself. Show students how experienced writers have a go by speaking aloud, how we 'talk in our heads' and how we overcome potential frustrations.

Then give students a topic to discuss and a keyword to repeat and add detail around as they experiment. For example, if students are discussing a view that homework should be abolished, they might try repeating say, 'effort'.

Ask them to use a similar structure to an example you give, such as, 'I know homework is a frequent and difficult job, but the effort required to do it requires an equal effort to avoid its completion'. Encourage a few attempts until students can hear when an effect is achieved.

Teaching tip

Try using the term 'amplification'. It can help students see the point of the technique: amplifying (or emphasising) the key term or point being made. Some students enjoy using a technical term for language effects.

IDEA 60

Beginning, middle and end

'This is for any teacher wanting to do some simple but effective work on sentences.'

If you don't have much time but you want a quick exercise for reminding students about sentence structure, this idea might help.

In this exercise, students try to build clear sentence structures in pairs. Here's how:

- Step 1: Explain the activity to your students and tell them what their sentence should be about. Keep it simple. It might be: 'Describe to your partner the journey from your tutor room to here.'
- Step 2: Student A starts a sentence. They tell it to a partner, Student B. Student A stops mid-sentence and passes the sentence on to their partner.
- Step 3: Student B continues the journey.
- Step 4: Student B passes it back to Student A who finishes it.

Now, try adding more challenge, such as:

- Don't allow the word 'the' at the beginning of the sentence. This encourages the use of subject-specific nouns or active verbs early in the sentence.
- Ask an examination-type question to prompt the sentence build.
- Use the start of a sentence from a high-grade examination response.

> **Teaching tip**
>
> Students might complete the pair work using the sentence continuation prompt cards (see online resources). These cards help build an argument or persuade someone, so adapt the subject of the sentence accordingly. For example: 'What you need to remember when you're heading for the lesson' (i.e. their attitude, being organised and helping others feel safe and valued).

IDEA 61

Joining two sentences

'This is for any class teacher. It's a five-minute activity that gets students to think about writing short sentences. Just noticing the sentences they've written is helping students' literacy.'

If you can spare the occasional five minutes to focus on building sentence skills, you slowly develop students' language skills. It helps students become more effective at expressing nuanced ideas and better at handling examination questions.

This activity takes five minutes. But in those few minutes, you will have done three things:

- asked students to reflect on language
- had students reflect on language effectiveness
- asked them to make choices about language.

These are key in the development of most students' language skills.

The activity is simple. Show two sentences. It's better if they're from a text you're using in the lesson, then:

- Ask students how they *might* be joined.
- Ask students if they *should* be joined.

Offer a few suggested conjunctions, such as, 'this is because', 'however', 'despite this' to make the connections. It's incremental steps like these that can grow students' grammatical repertoire.

Teaching tip

If you choose two sentences from different parts of the text, you might offer up surprising ways of linking cause, effect or process.

IDEA 62

Linking ideas, encouraging precision

'If you're getting students to do some comparative writing, try warming them up with a reminder of comparison words.'

This ten-minute activity helps students think about precision. There are fine differences between comparison words that add up to the richness and diversity of language.

Examiners find that students need help in drawing comparisons. Take this example from the 2015 AQA examiners' report on GCSE physics, chemistry and biology: 'Students could not **link ideas** and apply knowledge to different situations, for example, compost heaps have **the same** principle **as the** natural process of decay'.

To help your students link ideas more effectively, try the following:

- Choose five to ten students and give one word to each of these students from the comparison words card set (see online resources).
- Choose any two objects in the room, e.g. a table and the clock.
- Get the ten students to stand in a line facing the class and show the comparison word cards.
- Now ask the class to describe any similarities between the table and the clock. The challenge is to make any link. Usually there's at least one feature of any object that's similar to another.
- Every time someone uses one of the comparison words, the student holding the card sits down. The idea is to try and use all the words.
- What happens is that students will experiment with unfamiliar words and this is the point of the exercise. It's a safe and easy way of trying a range of linking words.

Teaching tip

Straight after, do lesson work that requires comparison. Stick the cards you've just used up around the whiteboard for reference.

IDEA 63

One word leads to another

'This is a bit of an advanced technique. I'd use it to teach the most able students who like a challenge. See what students can make of it.'

This device offers students a chance to discuss cause and effect. The writer or speaker repeats a word from the end of a sentence clause at the beginning of the next.

This is a challenge activity. Some students, not just the most able, enjoy playing with difficult language techniques.

- Give students a chance to experiment with sentences that use this technique. For example:
  - *The river becomes a sea. The sea becomes an ocean and the ocean gives life to all.*
  - *Colour is the breath of art. Art gives life to a school and a school ensures imagination is a gift forever.*
- To achieve progress, students try it out. It may work straight away; it may require some repeated attempts. That's how most writers develop their craft.
- You might try it yourself, modelling it with the class. Some students benefit from seeing teachers have a go at writing forms to see if they work. You might ask some students to spend time developing the technique for the class. After ten minutes or so they might present their sentences to the class.
- You might offer students some examples from published work. Students could be asked to say what the effect is. Students might be asked to say what they think the writer wanted us to think or feel. For example:
  - 'They call for you: the general who became a slave; the slave who became a gladiator; the gladiator who defied an Emperor.' – from the film *Gladiator*.

Teaching tip

You might want to give the rhetorical term for this: 'anadiplosis'. Some students enjoy knowing they've used a technique known to writers and speakers over many years.

Taking it further

You might set this as a homework challenge and you could get a small group to work together on it. Then they show you what they've been working on without performing it in front of the rest of the class. It's having a go that can make a difference.

IDEA 64

The order of things

'There are different ways of writing about what happens and when it happens.'

Show students the words for writing about the timing and ordering of events. Play with these words, experiment with them, and see what works and what doesn't.

This activity helps build students' fluency and ability to link events by time and cause. It will help your students learn to use conjunctions of time and place, for example, 'when', 'before', 'after', 'while', 'so', 'because' and adverbs such as 'then', 'next', 'soon', 'therefore'.

- Play word tennis with the timing grids (see the online resources). You use the first group. The students use the second. You take an event from the recent history of the lesson. You give the class a sentence and challenge them to give back a sentence using a word from the second group. You give a third sentence with another word from the grid. They give a fourth and so on. You win if they 'drop the ball' by repeating a word from the grid or not using one at all.
- Now get students to write about something that's happened in the recent past or something that happened today. They play word tennis in pairs.
- Or have students describe a process, trying to use at least three of the words in the card set. For example:
  - *Tell a partner about your journey to school.*
  - *Imagine giving a new student directions from the assembly hall to this classroom.*

Teaching tip

It will help English teachers if they try out the term 'adverb'. It also helps students link back to the work they did in primary school. Invite students to show the class how to use an online thesaurus to research similar words.

Taking it further

Ask students which three words they found the most useful and don't use ordinarily. Have them look back over their previous work and highlight words that have the same purpose. Have students use the same three words in their writing in the lesson or homework.

IDEA 65

Self-assessment quadrant

'I used this strategy to get students to think about their writing. It gives students a framework for reflecting on what they've written and how to improve it.'

This is a way of getting students to see the qualities needed in a piece of writing. Some students respond well to a diagrammatic approach as much as a list or chart. It's simply another way for students to plan and to bear the purpose of their writing in mind.

Give students the writing self-assessment quadrant (see online resources). It lists four qualities of good written work: **clear**, **accurate**, **detailed** and **thoughtful**. It asks students to list two or three features needed for each quadrant before they start writing. For example:

- **Clear:** Active voice, shorter sentences.
- **Accurate:** Use facts, use evidence, use quotes from the text.
- **Detailed:** Use the same number of details as points available for the question.
- **Thoughtful:** Use some of the phrases from the T cards (see Idea 68 and online resources).

The result is a plan for writing. It's more than a list of what to include and when. It helps students think about how to write as well as what to write. Students can then refer back to the quadrant after completing the piece of writing to reflect on what they've written and how it could be improved.

Teaching tip

When starting a piece of writing, ask the students to think which features will be most important. Single word answers don't require as much thought as an answer requiring a reason. Accuracy may not be as important in drafting work or planning. The grid can also be used to approach unfamiliar non-fiction writing. Students may decide that, for example, clarity may not be needed in deliberately misleading propaganda.

Taking it further

Ask students to invent or adapt the quadrant for another piece of writing or reading response. Thinking through the outcome in this diagrammatic form helps some students see the success criteria and envisage it when they set out their answer.

IDEA 66

Word limits

'Keeping to a word limit is such an important skill when students are getting ready for a test or exam.'

Here are some ideas for when you want to encourage students to keep to a word limit. Many students find quick language practice exercises most helpful. As with all practice, little and often is the guide.

Many of the following ideas are even more effective if the teacher models out loud the thinking a practised language user goes through.

- **Editing for redundancy:** Have students edit each other's writing so that only the most essential words are left. It's important they discuss the choices made.
- **Explain a scientific process in newspaper headlines:** For example, 'Class makes carbon dioxide by capturing expiration from plant'. Then edit this down to the most important four words.
- **One word explanations:** Everyone in the class is allowed one word only to sum up a historical figure.
- **Using the online thesaurus:** Try to reach consensus on the most important word for a geographical land formation. Get the words down to three and haggle from there. Done to a deadline, we're simulating the pressured thinking of an examination situation.
- **The cost of a word:** Try giving pupils an imaginary £10 word budget. Set the cost per word according to the ability of the group. See if they can make a profit. Summarise a text or write an introduction or a conclusion spending as little 'money' as possible while communicating with clarity and sense.
- **Six-word summary:** Ask students to summarise a whole text in six words. These

---

Teaching tip

It's surprising how much can be said in one minute. Have students time each other and try to say as much as they can in one minute. Many students would prefer to have a fairly straightforward activity, for example, 'So, look around the room. You have one minute to list all the objects you can see.' Or, 'List all the objects that have been made in a factory.' Or, 'List all the objects that can be lifted by one person.'

could be the most important six words from the text. Or express the text using six words of your own. Or explain the text in a complete sentence lasting no more than six words.
- **Word auction:** Students are given ten tokens to spend at a word auction. You offer students a text with five words missing and ten alternative words. Groups plan their spending strategy and the auction begins. You offer the words for sale and groups make bids.
- **Group edit:** Students start with a 30-word description of a process relevant to the lesson content and have one minute to edit it down. They pass it to the next group who have a further minute and then it's passed on again.
- **Cloze activity:** Offer, say, a scientific process containing only the nouns. Students have a time limit to add only the grammatical words – and as few as possible of them!

Taking it further

Ask students to imagine and describe something to a deadline. For example, 'In one minute, describe the last classroom you were in. Do this in the present tense, guiding the listener.' Or, 'In one minute, describe the classroom you're going to next.' Or, 'Show your partner your pen. In thirty seconds, describe it without looking at it.'

IDEA 67

The 'the' challenge

'You don't have to begin a sentence with the word "the". It's quite a revelation to some students.'

Using adverbs, verbs or nouns to begin sentences helps a writer 'get to the point' of a sentence quickly. This can be useful to remember when a student is writing examination answers.

Teaching tip

You might tell students 'the' is 'the definite article' and 'a' is the 'indefinite article'. Have students think of a sentence about their school day that starts with the definite article and see if it's interchangeable with the indefinite article. So, for example: 'The best thing about the school day is science.' This will change, with a slight modification to, 'A great thing about school is science.' So, the definite article helps us point to a single cause, effect or reason. The indefinite article helps when we want to leave room for alternatives.

Try this activity to help students practise starting sentences with words other than 'the':

- Student A tells their partner, Student B, about what's on their desk.
- Student B's job now is to notice how many times Student A issues a different word to begin the sentence.
- Change over. This time, Student A challenges Student B, 'You can only use the word "the" twice when you start a sentence.' Why? Because it means you're telling your partner about what you see and you're probably getting to the point more quickly.
- If you're not using 'the' you're probably beginning your sentence with a verb, an adverb or a noun.

You can develop this into a memory game:

- Have Student A assemble four objects on their desk. Student B tries to memorise them. Student B turns away and, without looking, says what's on the desk.
- Again, have students notice how they start their sentences. Did students use or omit the word 'the'?
- The real point here is to get students to notice efficiency. How quickly they make their point is a critically important literacy skill under exam conditions. I call this 'mindful literacy'. *Noticing* what's going on in language, trying to be *non-judgemental* and having a *wise relationship* with your writing.

IDEA 68

T cards

'The T cards help students get to the edge of their language comfort zone. There are words they know and words they don't.'

I developed these thinking cards to expand students' vocabulary, to challenge them and to get them to independence. I see them as scripts. They are prompts to help you learn your lines and play a scene in which you are an effective thinker.

The T cards are available in the online resources. Each card set is based on Bloom's taxonomy. Here's how you can use them:

- Print each group of words as a set or display them in their groups on your whiteboard.
- Allocate one set to each group.
- Ask the group to choose as many words as they can for a discussion.
- Tell them that they don't have to write anything to begin with.
- Then ask them, for example, to discuss a key aspect of the lesson.
- In their discussion, see how many of the words they can use.

Alternatively, you can use one card set and give each student the same for a specific lesson. Or, use two sets and have half the class use one and half the other. I find it useful when I vary their use in this way.

Taking it further

Print the cards on exercise book-sized paper so students can stick them in their books, turn the page and flip back and forth as they write. By looking and covering, they are beginning to commit words to memory. This simple, cheap method is so powerful. It takes seconds for students to look at a couple of words, perhaps trying them out by speaking them in sentences to their partner before using them in writing.

IDEA 69

C scripts – try before you buy

'I say to my literacy leader, "pass round the C scripts" and it just becomes a regular part of the lesson.'

In daily classroom work, students find it useful if they have a range of language types at their disposal. It's possible that the richer the language, the more chance there is of interesting ideas emerging. This activity provides students with a set of conjunctions to use in written tasks.

Use the C scripts (see online resources) to present students with a set of conjunctions they could use in written work. Explain to the class that the words in red are challenging, those in green help produce imaginative writing and the words in black are frequently seen. Print the A4 list or turn some or all of the words and phrases into playing cards or script sheets set out in play format – the simpler the better.

Model the words and phrases by role playing a scenario like the following:

- *You are trying to encourage a student who lacks self-confidence.*
- *You are a student asking for help from a teacher.*
- *You are a new student asking for help from a peer on their first day.*
- *You are a new teacher asking another teacher what they like about the school.*

Students then try this out in pairs. Saying and hearing new vocabulary before you write it down ('try before you buy') can help confidence.

Taking it further

Try modelling how to write a few sentences using the scripts. The students discuss how many of the phrases were effective. Almost always, effectiveness can be defined as what the audience feels, imagines, thinks, feels or is asked to do.

IDEA 70

C scripts – writing

'C scripts became a regular part of my teaching. I noticed that the words were used in high-grade GCSE scripts from various subjects.'

In writing for exams, students need to keep in mind an audience. This activity is a 20-minute refresher in using high-grade conjunctions for a real audience. It's a good lead into exam practice and helps students 'warm-up' their ability to write with nuance and imagination.

To practise writing for an audience, have students write on their own or with others short pieces for someone else to read. Give each group a different assignment. They write for another group in the class. Make sure they know which group they're writing for and they keep those students in mind when they write.

First, use the words on the C scripts (see online resources) to create a card showing a list of conjunctions the group must use in their writing. Get a literacy leader to give out a different C card to each group.

One member of each group then comes up to you. You give them their writing assignment. Think for a moment before passing it over, saying, 'I think you'll be good at this one. You're writing for group B, those students in the far corner. They are writing for you.'

The following are possible assignments for this activity that can be used in any subject:

- *Persuade another group that schools should or should not be open from 7am till 7pm.*
- *Describe a historical period you'd like to visit and why.*
- *Write a short speech for the head girl or boy that welcomes new parents and children to your school.*

Teaching tip

Explain to students that to be effective, their writing should encourage the reader to feel, think, imagine or take some sort of action.

Bonus idea ★

Try getting your staff to have a go at these. It can be a good way to get them introduced to the C scripts and possibly to get staff to think about conjunctions and adverbs that students could use in their subject area.

IDEA 71

The power of alliteration

'Starting words with the same letter can help students remember events in history, formulae in mathematics or a scientific process.'

This is a five-minute activity to help students sum up what is being learned. Using alliteration to do this helps students write brief summaries and can make a key aspect of the lesson memorable.

Alliteration doesn't have to be complicated to be effective. Even two words help. If you aren't an English teacher, don't worry. This is one of the most commonly taught language tricks. Students will know it from Key Stages 1 and 2.

Explain to students that the key with newspaper headlines is that they are designed to attract attention, make a sale and summarise succinctly (this is exactly what we need if we want lesson content to be memorable). Then ask students to make a newspaper headline using alliteration. The headline should describe part of the lesson, e.g. a geographical process, a historical event or a chemical reaction.
It helps if students see the teacher having a go first. Students need to see that experienced users of language don't get it right first time.

The headlines can become a challenge. Ask students to use fewer than ten words or ask them to use no fewer than three alliterations. You can use an online letter generator to help, such as **www.randomlettergenerator.com**.

Teaching tip

It helps if you have a few alliterative newspaper headlines from today's news to show students. Or you might offer some examples of alliteration from public and famous figures. The following examples show that alliteration doesn't always mean the same letter words have to be right next to each other:

'Let us go forth to lead the land we love.'
– John F. Kennedy

'My style is public negotiations for parity, rather than private negotiations for position...'
– Jesse Jackson

IDEA 72

The power of simile

'I find it helpful if I'm teaching about history, PSHE or science, to get students to use comparison in their writing. It helps them express an idea and to think imaginatively.'

This is a quick activity to help students to make a comparison using the word 'like'. It's a simple way of reminding them that sometimes we can express a personal response to an event, texture, musical idea, taste or colour.

Start by offering a few example similes and have students decide which is the more effective. For example:

- 'Character is like a tree and reputation its shadow.' – Abraham Lincoln
- 'He had electric blue hair that had stuck around his head like tendrils of a startled octopus.' – Cassandra Clare
- 'The water made a sound like kittens lapping.' – Marjorie Kinnan Rawlings
- 'A room without books is like a body without a soul.' – Marcus Tullius Cicero
- 'A mind is like a parachute. It doesn't work if it is not open.' – Frank Zappa
- 'It was a smooth silvery voice that matched her hair. It had a tiny tinkle in it, like bells in a doll's house.' – Raymond Chandler

Then try getting them to come up with their own similes to describe something related to the lesson content. Successful comparison needs experimentation, so have students discuss the feature they're comparing in partners, using the words 'like', or phrases such as 'it's almost like' and 'it is as if'.

Teaching tip

Many students will know the word 'simile' from Key Stage 2 work, so it helps them to link with this. Some students enjoy hearing teachers use shared language from different phases and in different subjects.

IDEA 73

The power of metaphor

'I'm always looking for ways to help students express an idea differently. When I encourage them to think about metaphor, it gives them a chance to say something new.'

By comparing a sound, a colour, a texture or a process with something else, students might express a nuanced idea. We might want to encourage this sort of response to develop a student's personal response to a text, a fabric, a piece of music, an historical event and so on.

Teaching tip

It's essential to make sure students know that effort is everything. An idea might come. Or it might not. The most important thing is having a go.

Students experience art, music, historical events and geographic forces differently to one another. Sometimes, the expression of their thoughts, feelings or ideas through comparison adds to students' deeper understanding. For example: 'The chord is ghostly.' 'The surface is lunar.'

One way of teaching this is to have students suggest comparisons through questioning and without too much self-criticism. Students can stumble on a thought that seems right to them this way. For example:

- *So, if Winston Churchill was a mountain, what would he be? (A river? A colour? A temperature? An animal?)*
- *If this fabric was a flower, what would it be? (A food? A sound? A landscape? An animal fur?)*

When finding more possible comparisons, try opening up the online thesaurus. 'So, if the storm was a creature, what would it be?' If you want more comparison ideas, type in 'creature' and you find: 'animal', 'beast', 'brute', 'living thing', 'living entity', 'living soul', 'soul', 'mortal', 'being', 'life form', 'organism'. If you want more, just enter one of the words and see where it takes the students' ideas.

You could offer a few examples, such as the following, and ask students to tell you what effect the writer has created:

- 'From Stettin in the Baltic to Trieste in the Adriatic, an iron curtain has descended across the continent.' – Sir Winston Churchill
- 'The torch has been passed to a new generation of Americans.' – John F. Kennedy

Taking it further

Ask the students to use the term 'metaphor' when they are developing their ideas.

IDEA 74

The rule of three

'I like rules that mostly work. I offer them as a sense of security to students in their speaking and writing, and they can also look out for them in their reading.'

In GCSE examinations, the highest marks are frequently given for using language for 'effective control of meaning' (Ofqual). Students might like to experiment with what's sometimes referred to as 'the rule of three'. This means giving, for example, three examples of a process, three reasons for a decision or three causes of an outcome.

Teaching tip

In formal rhetoric, the rule of three is known as the 'tricolon'. Some students enjoy knowing the technical terms for language they have tried. You might simply offer the term, just so they know there's a tradition to which they are connecting.

In class discussions, ask students to use phrases such as:

- There are three reasons for this…
- There are three unintended outcomes…
- Finally … [give three summary points].

Then analyse how convincing it is to use these phrases. Explain to students that the rule of three suggests a weight of evidence, which can help a reader be convinced of an explanation, argument or opinion.

If you have time, perhaps offer the following or other examples to students:

- 'Government of the people, by the people, for the people.' – President Abraham Lincoln
- 'Never in the field of human conflict has so much been owed by so many to so few.' – Sir Winston Churchill

Some students will have heard these sentences. It helps, sometimes, to know this device has been used for effect by others.

IDEA 75

Punctuation for all

'This is for any subject teacher. It's a quick way to get students to notice their punctuation. So often in teaching literacy this is the first step: noticing or paying attention to what you've written.'

Some students need occasional reminders of the importance of punctuation and this activity uses the content of the lesson. It is quick and can be used as a lesson starter or plenary.

- Ask students to read their work to a partner, speaking the punctuation marks aloud. Have them say the word 'full stop', 'comma' and so on.
- Next, have students read their work without saying the punctuation marks.
- The partner says 'pause' or raises their hand when they think a punctuation mark has been written.
- Have students test out the so-called 'three line rule' as they read their work. The 'three line rule' is just that. It reminds students to ask, every three lines of their page, whether they need to end the sentence. Some students use it to remind themselves when to use a full stop.

Taking it further

Students can devise an alternative to the 'three line rule' as a personal reminder for bringing sentences to an end.

IDEA 76

Subject – Time – Event – Place – Suspense (STEPS)

'What if I don't have much time but I want to help students with paragraphing?'

I find the STEPS acronym to work wonders when teaching paragraphing. It's short and memorable — after all, paragraphs are like steps on a page and form steps in a piece of writing.

Explain to students that paragraphing helps a reader to follow your thinking. Knowing how to separate out ideas can also help in examinations. Sometimes, a new paragraph means you're securing a new mark.
So, paragraphs can be very short.

Have students use this acronym to help them understand paragraphing: **STEPS**. Writers start a new paragraph when they do the following:

- **S** = When you change **Subject** or idea
- **T** = When **Time** changes
- **E** = When there is a different **Event**
- **P** = If you write about a new **Place**
- **S** = If you want to create **Suspense**

To put this into practice:

- Take a short piece of text with no paragraphs. Have students decide if there is a change in its 'STEPS'.
- Give each student a different STEP to notice. Don't worry that some may not feel they've found anything. That's important. The key is to get students looking closely at a text, noticing some of its features.
- Finally, have students self-assess writing in their books. Have them use colour coding to mark the changes in paragraph using a different colour for each of the STEPS they find.

> **Teaching tip**
>
> I use an extract from Malala Yousafzai's speech to the UN General Assembly because I want students to notice the power of the content. Paying attention to how it is written helps us pay attention to what is written. The speech is available here: www.un.org/News/dh/infocus/malala_speech.pdf

> **Bonus idea** ★
>
> **Have students write a short three-part description of a recent sporting or artistic success. They read this to a partner. Their partner tells them where they think the paragraphs have come. It introduces a new element to paragraphing in their own writing: pausing for dramatic effect.**

IDEA 77

Dance or mime the facts

'You could use dance or mime to offer students a memorable reading experience. This can work as an optional homework activity.'

There may be students in the class for whom dance and mime are an important method of response to an idea, thought or process. They rarely have the chance outside of PE, dance and drama to use the form. When other students see what has been created, the stimulus text can be made even more memorable.

The class have read a text in your lesson. When you're setting homework based on the text, offer the following activity as a 'wild card' choice. (You could have a set of 'wild cards' in envelopes that you give out when students ask. It helps make homework a bit more intriguing.)

- Suggest something like, 'Some of you are good at dance and mime. As your reading homework, why not turn the text into a dance? Or a sequence of mime moves? When the homework is due, present your dance or mime to the class.'
- The students pick out the music they want to go with the text and can perhaps even be inventive with the lighting in the classroom. The effect can be strong with, say, two balanced-arm lamps or a single Bunsen burner on the teacher's bench. As a backdrop, students might have the reading text displayed on the whiteboard and they perform in front of it and 'through' it.

Teaching tip

Have other students write a review of the dance presentation. Stress it must be positive. Ask them to describe what they saw. Ask them to say how it links to the reading text. The chances are high that for some students, when they are revising the text for a test or recalling it in the examination, it will be made more memorable because of the presentation.

Taking it further

Have the dance group set four questions about the text they're reading for the class to answer. It's the privilege of being brave. They have the right to get the class to think and respond.

IDEA 78

Hotseating

'This is a way of making reading content memorable. You can also get a high degree of focus by getting a student or yourself to play the content and invite questions from the class.'

Hotseating can help students read a text closely. They are going to ask questions to a character, writer, inventor, scientist or technologist. They might even quiz an object, process, art form or physical force.

Ask students to read a text used in the lesson, then work in groups to hotseat the content. Each group has:

- **A student in the hot seat:** This is a student in role as, for example, a character, a person from history, an inventor or an abstract concept from the text.
- **A questioner:** The student asking the questions.
- **A chairperson:** The student giving feedback to the group.

Each group thinks up two questions. They practise hotseating in their group, with the questioner asking the questions and the student in the hot seat answering them in role. The group then present the hot seating to the rest of the class.

Get the rest of the students to prepare some questions before the activity. Put them in a question box. Get the chairperson to pull the questions out. This makes sure that everyone takes part and gets their questions asked.

Teaching tip

If you want more control over the activity, you could be the questioner. Have each student in the room write a question and place it in a box. Take them out one by one to pose the questions. This allows you to control and edit them as you pick them out. Some may need 'tweaking' to help relate more clearly to the text.

IDEA 79

Analyse the diagram

'This activity gets students to think about the concept of analysis. It's so important sometimes to stop and pay attention to words we use so often in learning.'

Some students find it helps if they read for a purpose. In this activity we have students read and present information to help it become memorable for another group in the class.

Choose a text, diagram, chart or image that's key to the focus of your lesson. It might be something students need to remember for a test or examination. Have students read the text or look at the diagram and then teach it to another group in the class. Say to students, 'Analyse the diagram for another group. This means: break down the diagram into its constituent parts. Look in depth at each part. How does the process work? Present your analysis to an audience group.'

You could model the process first using an example from the lesson. Show students what you would look for. Show students that when you analyse you look at the relationships between the constituent parts.

Then students write a short analysis paragraph on the text or diagram in their books, pass it to a partner and get feedback on it, possibly by a comment shared at the end of the lesson. The partner can say which parts of the analysis they can recall. The analysis might be verbal. It might be another diagram, a chart or a graph. Say to students, 'Present your analysis in any way you choose. What do you think will help the reader?'

Teaching tip

Add a new level of challenge by requiring students to include a 'thinking register' in their analysis. Use the set of T cards (see online resources) to help. Show the students that you would make choices between different words. Model for students how you'd try out words to see if they fit.

IDEA 80

Dragons' Den

'I use this TV format when I want to encourage close reading. It helps students to look for reasons why the text should be read, why the content is important and its "unique selling point".'

In this activity, students present the content of a text as a pitch to a group of 'dragons' in the style of the TV show *Dragons' Den*. They might use the activity to prepare for a written précis of the text or they might be revising it for an exam and need it to be memorable.

Have students present the content of a text as a pitch to a group of 'dragons'. Students might have different sections of the same text to present. Sometimes I play the presenter role or get another student to lead this. I always begin the activity with the TV theme tune.

For the presentation:

- Students use scanning skills to find the most important parts of the text.
- They use skimming skills to present the outline content of the text.
- They use inference skills to persuade the 'dragons' about the text's purpose.
- The 'dragons' are another peer group. They ask their questions either verbally or using sticky notes, writing their questions down and passing them to you to read out. This makes sure that everyone gets involved.
- The presentation includes a 'unique selling point'. This might be a list of the most important things to remember for an exam, how the text explains a scientific method, the most important features of an historical event or the main themes of a poem. The students present the summary persuasively.
- Students say things to the 'dragons' like: 'Here's why you should read this text' or, 'This text might change your life'.

Teaching tip

You can use the sticky notes to pass the questions round different groups. This makes sure the most helpful questions get shared. You can also add core questions of your own to ensure challenge.

Taking it further

The 'dragons' are experts in their field. Give each 'dragon' a specialism relating to the lesson content and ask them to find one new fact about it. In this way, you're growing content and the skill of questioning.

IDEA 81

Plenary page

'Plenary page helps make writing important. It's to do with having a routine of feedback between the student and me. The CQL technique can be varied to suit you and your class and can be personalised by the student so it becomes their own version. It works in any lesson.'

Writing a learning summary to the class teacher as a real audience helps encourage accuracy. The writing isn't going to be judged. It's an act of communication. The Sutton Trust found that reflection on learning can help student progress.

- Ask students to leave a space of say ten lines at the start of the next page in their exercise books. Doing this makes it more likely you'll remember to return to it whenever you do the plenary action.
- Title it 'Plenary'. Students complete it at any time that makes sense to you. It need not be at the end of the lesson.
- Students put three letters down the side of the space: C Q L. These prompts encourage three different sentences:
  - **C:** Students write the **Content** of the lesson that's stuck most successfully.
  - **Q:** They ask a **Question** that's arisen during the lesson.
  - **L:** They make a comment about how they've **Learned**, i.e. which learning activity helped the most (the practice test, the drama, the group discussion, etc.).

You can access the Sutton Trust's Teaching and Learning Toolkit here: www.suttontrust.com/about-us/education-endowment-foundation/teaching-learning-toolkit.

Teaching tip

Many students find it effective over time to reflect on how they've learned. For example, writing out how they learned to spell or how they solved a mathematics question can make it more likely they'll be successful next time. In this way, the plenary pages become feedback logs.

IDEA 82

Ambassador oracy

'This activity will help you give some structure to speaking. You simply get your class to tell another class what they've been learning. It can be done in ten minutes.'

Telling someone who hasn't been in the lesson what has been learned can help make the content become memorable. Plan this activity with a colleague who teaches in a room in the same corridor, preferably next door or opposite.

- Partner with a teacher who teaches close by to you.
- Agree a time for the activity to start, say 2pm.
- Both of you give each student one of two letters: A or B.
- At 2pm, all the letter As swap classes and sit in the places vacated by the other letter As.
- The letter As tell the Bs they are now sat next to one of the most important things they have learned this lesson.
- The Bs tell the As the same, that is, the most important thing they have learned this lesson.
- The As now return to their 'home' classroom. They report to their 'home' Bs what they've just heard.
- Teach students the manner of greeting you require. They'll need this when they pass their 'ambassador' partners in the corridor as they swap places. They use it again as they greet their B partners in their 'guest' classrooms.

Taking it further

Instead of swapping classrooms, the students can write messages, hand them in to you to edit and then pass to the partner teacher for her/his class. When the messages are read, you can require a question comment. This must aim to deepen understanding. You can use the stem question sheet (see the question scripts in the online resources).

IDEA 83

Preparing for a learning walk – literacy

'If a school leader is coming to your lesson, they're looking at learning and safeguarding. So, keep it simple and only do a literacy activity if it fits your intended learning outcomes.'

You shouldn't do anything different if you're being visited. All learning visits should help students' learning. When helping students develop literacy skills, focus on the skills that help them achieve success in your subject.

Don't do anything different if you're being visited by a colleague. Use the visit to emphasise to students the importance of accurate literacy. Don't do anything over complicated. Most students prefer things made simple and straightforward.

You might try some of the following:

- Have students correct their spelling mistakes.
- Have them rewrite a paragraph or sentence so it makes more sense. (Use whatever colour pen they are used to.)
- After pair discussion, spend a minute or two getting them to improve their vocabulary. Ask them to use one or more subject-specific words in their talk.
- Ask students to spend a moment thinking about what makes good listening in your subject. They might come up with a golden rule.
- Have students tell someone else in their group about a book they found helpful in your subject, whether it is fiction or non-fiction.

Teaching tip

Model for students the way you write. Think out loud while you're at the whiteboard. Consider two or three ways of starting a sentence. Tell students what goes through your mind when you're thinking about punctuation and when you think about spellings. How do you bear in mind the audience you are writing for?

Taking it further

Students edit a piece of writing they did last week. Ask them to think about how it might help them write more clearly, which punctuation might have helped, whether there are sentences that need to be shorter, how rich the vocabulary is and if the tone is formal enough.

Part 8

Lessons – maths

IDEA 84

The Frayer grid

'This simple grid helps students learn key mathematical words. If you use it occasionally, it keeps its value. Think about the six most important words students need to use in a half term.'

This simple technique, if used regularly, teaches students how to learn key mathematical vocabulary independently.

Teaching tip

The grid is particularly useful for homework. It can be used to get pupils to research independently or in pairs. It's better if they fill in the boxes themselves, making mistakes as they go. They correct them with you when they return it. Improving from trial and error helps secure the learning.

This is an outline of the Frayer grid (see online resources for a larger, printable version):

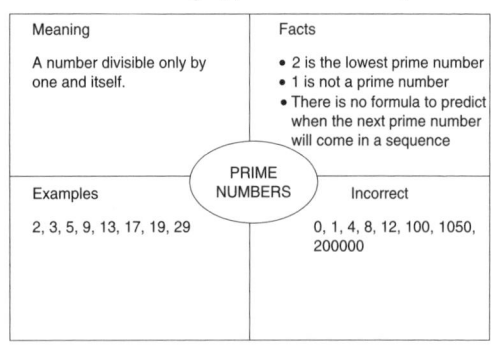

Meaning	Facts
A number divisible only by one and itself.	• 2 is the lowest prime number • 1 is not a prime number • There is no formula to predict when the next prime number will come in a sequence
Examples	Incorrect
2, 3, 5, 9, 13, 17, 19, 29	0, 1, 4, 8, 12, 100, 1050, 200000

(Centre: PRIME NUMBERS)

Here's how to use it:

- Students put a keyword in the centre of the box.
- Top left: they write a definition.
- Top right: students add some facts about the keyword.
- Lower left: they add some examples of the keyword.
- Lower right: they put some examples of what the keyword is not.

IDEA 85

Comparison in mathematics

'A really simple and quick activity for mathematics teachers.'

Comparison is often key in mathematics lessons. Although students tend not to write as much prose in mathematics, it helps students to see how comparison skills transfer between subjects.

This is a quick exercise that draws attention to language while learning mathematics. Learning in both subjects is helped.

Take three contrasting terms from the mathematics curriculum. For example:

- An **acute angle** is an angle less than 90°.
- An **obtuse angle** is an angle between 90° and 180°.
- A **reflex angle** is an angle between 180° and 360°.

Students then work in threes:

- Student 1 makes a **statement** about the acute angle.
- Student 2 **compares** acute angles to obtuse angles using a conjunction.
- Student 3 makes a **contrasting** statement comparing both acute and obtuse angles to reflex angles.

Create some comparison playing cards to speed up the exercise and support word choice. Have your literacy leader give them out to save you time.

Then try a speed challenge. See if students can do this in two minutes.

Taking it further

Show examples of the use of adverbials in work from high-grade pieces of writing.

IDEA 86

Mathematics reading

'This is for a mathematics teacher who wants to get students reading closely.'

As a mathematics teacher, you might want to teach students the importance of reading closely. Setting a reading task in mathematics can be an efficient way of supporting the school's literacy project.

For students, there's an important link to be made between reading closely in English and in mathematics. In this activity, they see a mathematics text as reading material without having to answer questions:

- Ask students to read a few sample examination questions and tell them that they are going to write their own. Ask students to think of three 'rules' that govern the questions they've read. For example:
  - *Write 0.38 as a percentage.*
  - *Write 36% as a fraction in its simplest terms.*
  - *Write three hundred thousand in figures.*
- If necessary, prompt with (for example):
  - They are commands.
  - They begin with verbs.
  - There are no adjectives.
  - No sentence begins with 'the'.
  - They are short.
- Ask each student to invent an exam-style question about anything students genuinely want an answer to. The point is that the questions are then *really* going to be read.
- Collect them in. Tell students that you're going to send them off to a real audience, students in another class, for example, and if possible, have the real audience answer them.

Taking it further

You might make regular contact with the mathematics department at your local college or university. The UK has a programme called 'Aimhigher'. Going through this link can help you get access to a university's outreach programme. Having, say, an annual Skype call projected into the classroom with teachers and students at a local university, offers aspiration opportunities. Have students prepare questions about the value of learning mathematics in a post-18 setting.

IDEA 87

Mathematics vocabulary grid

'This simple vocabulary grid helps students remember key terms they need. It's useful in other subjects too.'

Sometimes, very simply, it helps to focus attention on the way we learn vocabulary. Use this vocabulary grid occasionally for the top ten or 15 words students are going to need in a fortnight.

Download and print copies of the vocabulary grid from the online resources.

At the start of the lesson, students complete the column, 'My definition before'. You encourage them to have a go rather than writing 'don't know'. But we want to avoid frustration. If 'don't know' helps confidence, then that's what the student writes.

Towards the middle of the lesson, the student writes what they think now in the column 'My definition after'. You may have taught the vocabulary or it may appear in the next lesson.

Next, the student anchors the word by writing it in a sentence in the final column. They do this a little time later or **as a homework**.

The grids might be shared on a class intranet so that everyone has access to different styles of presenting a variety of definitions. Suppose you had a vocabulary grid 'word bank' with a range of mathematical vocabulary written by a number of students, presented imaginatively. You might even invite parents to get access to help with homework and revision.

Teaching tip

Check the students grasp the meaning of the word. You may want to do this as a whole class, modelling what you would do if you got stuck. Have the students use the words in their test practice as soon as possible. The sooner students can feel they've got it right independently, the better.

Part 9

Lessons – science and technology

IDEA 88

'Thinking words' in science

'When I set regular homework about science language, I found it easier for students to make links between my subject and their English work. It encouraged confidence and skills in key terminology.'

In science examinations, especially the longer questions, students need to nuance their answers. In science lessons, students need to think in a variety of ways, making connections, evaluating and understanding, all steps in Bloom's Taxonomy.

Teaching tip

Choose an audience to read the students' work. Ideally it should be someone outside the class because when writing for examinations, students don't know the reader. In the example given here, you could send the students' pieces of writing to the European Space Agency education department, for example (**www.esa.int/Education**). Even if there's no guarantee they will get a reply, they have an incentive for ensuring accuracy.

Set this activity as a regular task, say once a month.

- Have the students read a text extract relating to the lesson content. You could choose an extract from this text about the International Space Station (published by the European Space Agency), for example: **esamultimedia.esa.int/images/edukit/english/Edukitchap1_E.pdf**.
- Model how to use the phrases on the T cards (see online resources). The students then interview you about the text as if you wrote it.
- Don't worry about this seeming artificial. The process of learning new language is often a process of trial and error in a safe setting. Students need to see writers thinking aloud.
- For about five minutes, using the T cards, students discuss a key aspect of the text, for example three features of the International Space Station that will help life on earth.
- Finally, show students how you would write three sentences making three separate points about the International Space Station (for example) and ask them to write their own for homework.

Send their writing to an audience outside the classroom to read. Invite the students to see what the audience thought in their response.

IDEA 89

Invent an element

'I'm a chemistry teacher. I want to draw attention to the importance of vocabulary but I can't spend much time on language skills. There's so much content to cover.'

Examiners in science say that a common mistake students make at GCSE is inaccurate use of specialist terms. This quick activity can help. The more you have a go at it, the more time efficient you become.

Have students invent a chemical element:

- First, they look at three elements from the periodic table. Since 1947, the International Union of Pure and Applied Chemistry (IUPAC) has had the responsibility for agreeing words for new elements. In this exercise, you are the IUPAC.
- If you have time, tell them that some elements are named after legends and myths (e.g. nickel and cobalt); some are named after the place (europium) or countries (americium, francium, polonium) where they were found.
- Tell students that there's an agreed code in the science community that all new elements end with the suffix 'ium'.
- Then, students invent one. They could:
  - name it after a place they know
  - name it after a mythical creature
  - name it after a quality, an emotion or a skill.
- Next, they describe it to a partner. How important is it? Will it help cure an illness, power a machine or speed up the Internet?
- Next, they write it in a sentence for its entry in the IUPAC scientific journal, *Pure and Applied Chemistry*.

The exercise has students gaining an understanding that language is as social and ever-changing as it is scientific, renewing their interest in learning and using specialist terms accurately.

Taking it further

Have students write a test question based on their element for a partner to answer. They give double marks for answers that contain the new element's name.

Bonus idea ★

Students read a question from a GCSE exam paper and identify any technical terms. As part of their homework, they search the derivation of the terms on the Internet. They offer the derivation to a partner as a follow-up activity in class. Can their partner guess the term?

… **IDEA 90**

Writing for clarity in science

'This is for science teachers who want to help students write more clearly.'

In 2016, AQA examiners in GCSE biology, chemistry and physics reported that students needed to improve their skills in writing clear answers because they 'gave vague answers with insufficient information'. We can help by simply drawing attention to words that improve clarity.

Taking it further

Have students use an online thesaurus to find alternative phrases of clarification and try them out in talk. Challenge students to try out new clarification words in talk and in writing over the next week.

List three steps in a process. The three steps in photosynthesis, for example, are:

- capturing energy from light
- using ATP and NADPH to power the synthesis of carbohydrates from CO_2
- using energy to make ATP and NADPH.

Then:

- Have students explain the steps to a partner.
- Next, reorder the steps.
- Have students explain what's changed and whether this is the scientifically correct order.
- Now offer three phrases of clarification from the clarification prompt cards (see online resources).
- Students talk through the scientifically correct order using any of the clarification phrases or new ones.
- Finally, they write out the process, underlining or highlighting the grammatical phrases that helped clarification.
- You might then have students highlight and underline phrases of clarification from an example answer in a test or examination.
- Have them suggest alternative phrases of clarification from the card sets.

IDEA 91

Sounding formal in science

'This is for teachers working on the six-mark answer. Sometimes, taking pronouns out of a sentence helps summarise scientific content.'

Using the passive voice removes opinion. This can be useful when writing objectively, for example, when presenting findings to an audience or in a science examination when students don't have much time.

- First, remind students what pronouns are, for example: he, she, I, we, they.
- Show them an example sentence that uses pronouns: 'Excess heat meant we had to make sure all the objects were cooled down and to take the heat away.'
- Show them how we can rewrite this to make it shorter and take away the pronoun: 'Excess heat meant the objects needed cooling.' ('Cooling' has been used to summarise 'cooled down and to take the heat away'.)
- Role play with volunteers. Choose any scientific process. For example:
  - 'In our group we used litmus paper to test the acidity or alkalinity of the fluid.' becomes: 'Litmus paper was used to test the acidity or alkalinity of the fluid.'
  - 'My partner and I had to make sure we tested the copper sulphate solution again.' becomes: 'The copper sulphate solution was tested again.'
- During the lesson, have students describe any part of the lesson and challenge them to do so without pronouns.
- You might have the class apply a writing efficiency test. Students set questions for each other about the work they have been doing. They challenge each other to answer in as few words as possible while still making complete sense. They try to avoid using pronouns.

Teaching tip

Show students a model text, for example:

'A solution is made when a solute, usually a soluble solid compound, is dissolved into a liquid called a solvent, typically water. If the solute is white (e.g. sodium chloride) then the solution is colourless.' (**www.bbc.co.uk/education/guides/zgbqtfr/revision**)

The simple challenge is to say how formal this sounds and how believable is reads. Can students spot any pronouns?

IDEA 92

T cards for exam preparation

'I used the T cards to get students practising examination-type answers. They were especially useful in the longer, six-mark, answers.'

In the six-mark answers, students have to write efficiently and use scientific language. It helps if students learn vocabulary that helps them write in the scientific method.

Teaching tip

The key is to do this activity little and often. Keep the structured practices short – 20 minutes is fine. After all, they won't get much time in the examination.

Students might try writing practice exercises. Suppose you provide them with an information diagram about photosynthesis from an examination sample paper. Students choose from the following activities or you choose for them. The activities are loosely based on the style of examination questions.

1. Explain the diagram for another group.
2. Clarify the process. Explain the specialist terms.
3. Analyse the diagram for another group. Break down the diagram into its constituent parts. Look in depth at each part. How important is each part?
4. Can you come up with an invention based on the diagram?
5. Evaluate the diagram. Reach a conclusion about the strengths and weaknesses of the diagram.
6. Examine the diagram. Look in detail and establish its key facts and any important issues arising from its content.

The students talk through their answers first:

- Start by giving each student the same T card (see Idea 68 and online resources). It helps concentration if they've got fewer words on which to focus.
- Model an answer. Try challenging students to choose the words you use from the T card. The aim is to show how you think.

- Next try writing sentences as answers. You write one sentence on the board. Students write the next. You write the final sentence.
- For the next answer, reverse this to grow independence: they write the first, you write the second and they write the final sentence.
- For the third answer, possibly for homework, the students write all three sentences.
- Challenge students to use unfamiliar words or phrases from the T cards.

Give them five minutes to write three sentences. Say to students that they should use at least one word or phrase from the T script card.

By doing this, you're helping students see there's always a purpose to writing and they should keep a reader in mind.

> **Bonus idea** ★
>
> You might reinforce the idea that writing should help a reader feel, imagine, think or take action. So, as a warm up, ask students to choose one of the following:
>
> 1. Persuade another student that schools should or should not be open from 7am till 7pm. To be effective, the writing should encourage the reader to feel, think, imagine or take some sort of action.
> 2. Invent a new earth element and explain its use, properties and possible applicability. To be effective, the writing should encourage the reader to feel, think, imagine or take some sort of action.
> 3. Describe an historical period you'd like to visit and why. To be effective, the writing should encourage the reader to feel, think, imagine or take some sort of action.

IDEA 93

Build the content

'This is for a technology teacher wanting to make a text memorable. I've used this when I've known there are students in my class who are skilled at construction.'

Students with skills in technology can see how to combine resources to make a shape or design that illustrates a process and helps them to remember it.

When students have to learn a process, a flow chart, or a diagram, suggest they build a representation of the content using whatever they can find in the room:

- Tell students they can only use what they can find on their desk or in the classroom and they can use no more than six items.
- Ask students to present their representation of the content to the rest of the class. Give them T cards (see Idea 68 and online resources) to help them do this. Say something like, 'When you present, justify your design to the audience group using at least four words or phrases from your T card.'
- You might want to role play the T card first so students get to hear some of the more unfamiliar phrases and words used properly.
- If you have time, have the students try a role play in pairs like the one you've just done. We want students to experiment with new vocabulary when the stakes are not as high as a test or examination.

Taking it further

You might take a scan of the build, if it will help them remember the process or flow chart. The build might be labelled using keywords. You might have enough accurate and helpful designs to create a photo montage for display or even for students' books.

Part 10

Lessons – art, drama, music and PE

IDEA 94

The punctuation party

'Students enjoy imagining what personalities punctuation marks might have. It gets them to think about what punctuation marks do.'

A drama exercise like this can help students talk about and remember the variety of punctuation marks and their different effects. After this exercise, it's likely that they'll think a little more about the functions of punctuation and perhaps even talk about it in social time.

This activity could be part of a drama lesson but it's especially useful if taught by the drama teachers to an entire year group.

- Show the students a punctuation pyramid (see online resources). Say to the class something like, 'Choose a punctuation mark from the pyramid but don't tell anyone what it is. Does anyone want to ask what any of these marks are?'
- Now students move round the room and meet and greet a partner. They invite their partner to guess what punctuation mark they thought of. I do this as an exercise in pretend telepathy. They send the punctuation mark out into the air of the classroom and their partner says what they see. It's surprising how many are right!
- Next students move around the room again and meet and greet another partner. This time, they are the punctuation mark. When they meet, suggest they say something like, 'Good morning. Great to meet you. I'm a full stop. I'm terribly important. There's lots of me around. I tell readers when a sentence has ended.'
- Now the students move around again and speak in the personality of their punctuation. Would it be confident or shy? Would it be welcoming or nervous?
- I play some party music during this – just to help everyone relax.

Bonus idea ★

Put a different text type in each corner of the room. For example: a science exam answer, an extract from *Harry Potter*, an extract from a geography text book and a newspaper article. Now ask students, still in role, to stand closest to the text type where they think they would be found. Students find themselves pulled between text types. When students think and discuss where they are likely to be found, they discover themselves learning about punctuation effects.

IDEA 95

Vocabulary in art

'Art teachers have so many resources to help students' literacy. Art helps words become visual, so they are seen in new ways and become memorable.'

Art teachers regularly extend students' vocabulary when they have students discuss the effect of media and technique choice. This activity uses art displays to enrich the process of word selection.

- Have students each think of three positive words to describe the school.
- Use 2−3−4 to get the words shared through the class. In this activity, students have **two** minutes to share their **three** words with **four** students (see Idea 49).
- Have students make a colour and texture montage of the words. Make sure the montages can be seen from a distance.
- Display them along the whole of a corridor wall, around the canteen servery or in the entrance to the school. Put word montages wherever students line up to go into their classrooms or around whiteboards. Both students who have created the montage and those who see them on their way to class will be more likely to remember and use them, extending their vocabulary.

Teaching tip

Upload the words to the school art department page on the school website. Art can help celebrate the literacy of the school.

IDEA 96

Punctuation in music

'Sometimes there is valuable literacy in an examiner's report. You'll find them in every subject.'

This activity helps combine writing for audiences, noticing what skilled writers do and learning about successful GCSE music answers. It's surprising how infrequently students get to see what examiners say about writing. Getting students to write as if they were examiners encourages them to read the content closely.

- Set a homework task for students that requires them to write a two-paragraph review of a download they've bought recently.
- Ask them to write like an examiner. This requires a brief look at how examiners write. In this example, the writer has been succinct. The writer achieved this by using clear examples to support ideas, commas. Most sentences are less than three lines and under 22 words long:

   'Compositions covered a wide range of styles and genres and candidates were able to demonstrate a good range of ability and technical awareness. Styles included string quartets, pop songs, programmatic music, pieces for solo piano and many others, usually making the most of pupils' experience of learning a particular instrument. Candidates who focused on genres and instrumentation they were familiar with did markedly better and were able to demonstrate a good level of understanding of the capabilities of the instruments and the style of the music.'
   CCEA GCE – Music, Summer Series 2016, Chief Examiner's Report

- Writing like an examiner helps students with their evaluative style. It also requires paying attention to the content, which obviously has a direct relevance.
- Circulate all the students' two-paragraph reviews in the class and ask for written responses.

Taking it further
You could also have another class read the reviews and write responses or publish some of the reviews on the school website.

Bonus idea ★
Invite a colleague in another school to have their students review the music of one of your school bands. Do the same for them. See if you can get students to generate interest in the music being produced at each other's schools.

IDEA 97

'Thinking language' in PE

'It helps if I model thinking language with the class and then quickly challenge them to experiment with it.'

PE GCSE, A level and BTEC examinations require students to explain their reasoning and to make links between processes.

- Ask literacy leaders to hand out the T cards (see Idea 68 and online resources).
- Demonstrate the phrases on the T cards with a role play. Model it with a volunteer. Role plays could be, for example:
  - Student A is a student new to the school. Student B explains what the school values and believes is a good way to behave.
  - Student A gives advice to Student B on how to succeed at school at building and maintaining friendships.
- The class checks how many phrases you used from the T cards. You try to get in as many as you can. Model what to do if you're not sure – try it anyway and ask whether it's correct.
- Then have the students work through a quick pair role play doing the same thing.
- If you're in a classroom, present an example letter written to a local newspaper. Draw attention to the beginning and the end, to the tone and to any phrases used from the T cards.
- Next have students think of some sports skills that young people need to develop in their own time, e.g. basic cardiovascular fitness, muscle strength and core strength. Have them decide what sports could help with this. For homework, they draft a short letter to their local newspaper with a request that the paper publishes their thoughts. They try to use no fewer than three phrases from the T cards.

Teaching tip

Students could read and respond to a partner's letter as if they were the manager of a local sports venue pointing out what's already on offer.

Taking it further

You might seek a response from someone external to the school. If you can, have them comment on the strengths of the way in which the letters were written and how formal they were. Ask them to say whether any of the thinking phrases helped make the case and what phrases get their attention when they read unsolicited mail.

Part 11

Lessons – PSHE and history

IDEA 98

Persuasion in PSHE

'I'm teaching PSHE this afternoon. How can I help students' persuasive writing? Can I get students to read using "real life" texts?'

Sometimes, students say they don't know how to get started on a written piece or how to write more. The writing grid in the online resources might help you. Use the vocabulary sets as cards or as projected displays. They are designed to help students emphasise a point or persuade a reader.

Teaching tip

Ask students to make their own versions of the writing grid for their exercise books. Use an online thesaurus to build the new vocabulary sets. Next to each new grid, students write a short paragraph using some of the words and phrases.

Bonus idea ★

Suggest students write in role to an audience drawn from one of the nine 'protected characteristics'. Invite students to search the gov.uk website on discrimination: www.gov.uk/discrimination-your-rights. After all, in PSHE, we want to encourage the kind of reading a participating and informed citizen might do. You might get students to use nationally available resources for a citizen wanting to help themselves or others promote equality of opportunity.

If students say they're stuck or don't know how to start a persuasive written piece, offer them the writing grid (see online resources). Show them how you'd use it and how you get more independent. The more you can write 'out loud' for students the better.

You might get students to use the vocabulary sets in role first. Get students into pairs. With the grid in front of them, choose, for example, one of the following:

- Student A persuades Student B that they can aspire to a career of their choice.
- Student B persuades Student A that they can pass any examination with effort and determination.
- Student A persuades Student B that it's worthwhile getting involved in the school council.

Now have them write short paragraphs with the grid turned over or hidden from display. Getting to this point shortly after writing and discussing helps increase independence. The subject could be: 'Celebrate the school's values of diversity', or 'Explain to a new entrant the virtue of hard work and effort, cooperation and tolerance.' Get them to read their work to a partner.

IDEA 99

Conjunctions in history

'I find it useful to show students the conjunctions that we can find in high-grade GCSE answers.'

High-band writing in history GCSE examinations requires students to use evidence convincingly. This activity devotes a few minutes to noticing and practising this use of language.

- Have students look back through their work or each other's work for conjunctions. Then show them the Grade 9 conjunction cards (see online resources). These are a set of cards with words and phrases to talk about cause and effect, taken from top-band answers in the OCR 2015 history exemplar writing pack.
- Ask students where they would travel to if they could go back in time.
- They describe their destination to a partner as if trying to sell it as a destination for time travel tourism. They use the cards as support.
- Ask them to write this description, telling them to remember that some writing aims to have the audience feel, imagine, think or do something.

Teaching tip

Send students' work to the education department of a local museum or art gallery. Ask them if they'll acknowledge receipt. They might do more, especially if they are displaying the work of local schools. Even if there's no certainty of a reply, it's helpful for students to know their work is going to be read by an external audience.

IDEA 100

Questions in PSHE

'Once I did this simple questioning activity, my teaching was never the same. It's literacy and learning completely aligned.'

What we're doing in this idea is helping students learn the language of question types, while showing them that the content of the lessons over the next half term will be shaped by our curiosity. This example is from a PSHE lesson, but change the content and it could be any lesson.

All you need for this activity is slips of paper and a box. You'll need some courage too.

- You might say to the class something like, 'I want you to help me plan the lessons for the next six weeks. I want to help answer the questions you might have. You can ask whatever you like. I'll check over the questions to make sure they're safe. But I won't know who wrote them – unless you want to tell me.'
- Let's suppose you're teaching about the NASA Curiosity mission to Mars. There are many sites with Curiosity-related content. Here's one with details of the Curiosity search for microbial life: **www.space.com**.
- Give each student a slip of paper and ask them to write a question about the mission. They write it and fold up the slip.
- You may need to model writing questions. You may need to lead with some content-based material to familiarise them with the subject.
- The question prompt resource (see online resources) has groups of questions. You give them out so there's different types of question round the room. Students can swap to get them thinking. This is the core literacy learning: the language of question types.

Teaching tip

You might devote a part of the classroom display to the questions raised. It helps if you can get the questions represented into a readable font size, but even if you don't, the sticky note display will be intriguing for students as they come into the classroom. Making it more lasting helps secure the sense that the learning is genuinely cooperative.

- Tell the students that over the next few weeks you'll have a go at answering all the questions. Tell them that you may not have the answers and if that's the case, 'We'll try to answer them together during our lessons over the next few weeks.'
- Collect the questions in a box making sure they are anonymous. You may find that because students don't have to say who wrote them, the questions are a little less inhibited.
- Of course, as you open each one to read it for the class, you'll have editorial control. Occasionally, a few questions may need amending.
- Display the questions. Have them typed up into a large font. Print them onto large sticky notes. Cluster them round your whiteboard. Keep referring to them as the weeks go by. Build them into your planning. Have some students chase down possible answers.
- Stress that there will certainly be more than one answer.

Taking it further

You might send the questions off to the European Space Agency's education department, the physics department of a local higher education institution or the A level physics class in your school and ask for a response. Remind students that even if there's no response, the act of asking questions helps promote learning.